THOMAS LINES is a freelanc‹ international agricultural working life as a journalis modity and financial markets ... London and Paris, and later became a lecturer in international business at Edinburgh University. He has worked as a team leader of agricultural aid projects and a policy advisor for UN agencies, leading NGOs, and fairtrade and trade union organizations.

The author has worked in more than 40 countries and speaks fluent French and Russian. He was a candidate for the Green Party in the 2005 UK general election.

His recent work as a research consultant made him look at world markets and their impact on poverty from numerous angles, according to his clients' requirements. This unusual wealth of experience leads the author to some troubling questions about the way the globalized economy affects the Earth's poorest inhabitants.

Eleanor Barreau March 2011

Making Poverty
A HISTORY

Thomas Lines

Zed Books

LONDON & NEW YORK

Making Poverty: A History was first published in 2008 by Zed Books Ltd,
7 Cynthia Street, London N1 9JF, UK and
Room 400, 175 Fifth Avenue, New York, NY 10010, USA
www.zedbooks.co.uk

Cover designed by Andrew Corbett
Interior designed and set in 11/12.5 pt Perpetua by Long House, Cumbria, UK
Printed and bound in Malta by Gutenberg Press Ltd

Distributed in the USA exclusively by Palgrave Macmillan, a division of
St Martin's Press, LLC, 175 Fifth Avenue, New York, NY 10010

A catalogue record for this book is available from the British Library

US Cataloging-in-Publication Data is available from the Library of Congress

ISBN 978-1-84277-941-5 hb
ISBN 978-1-84277-942-2 pb

Contents

List of Tables and Figure / vi
List of Abbreviations / vii
Foreword / ix

Introduction / 1

1 Those who have fallen behind / 5

2 How poverty is made / 29

3 Do the market's job for it / 61

4 Not farming but gambling / 93

5 Getting out of the trap / 118

6 Can we put history behind us? / 140

Bibliography / 150
Index / 160

Tables and Figure

Table 1 The countries with the highest human development indicators 10

Table 2 The countries defined as of low human development 12

Table 3 Average world primary commodity prices
over three-year periods, 1977–9 and 2004–6 40

Table 4 Changes in terms of trade of some country
groups, 1980–2 to 2001–3 43

Table 5 Commodity-dependent developing countries (2003–5)
grouped by the character of trade access to the US and EU of
their leading commodity export 74

Table 6 Vegetable trade in sub-Saharan Africa, 1990 and 2005 81

Table 7 Sub-Saharan Africa's trade in staple foods and sugar 121

Figure 1 Types of commodity supply management
(limiting supply) 87

Abbreviations

A&P	Great Atlantic & Pacific Tea Company
ACP	Africa, Caribbean and Pacific
AERC	African Economic Research Consortium
ASEAN	Association of South-East Asian Nations
c	(US) cent
CAADP	Comprehensive Africa Agriculture Development Programme (under NEPAD)
COMESA	Common Market for Eastern and Southern Africa
cu. m	cubic metre
DR Congo	Democratic Republic of Congo
EIC	East India Company
EU	European Union
EurepGAP	European Retailers' Protocol for Good Agricultural Practice
FAO	Food and Agriculture Organization of the United Nations
GATT	General Agreement on Tariffs and Trade
GCDS	Global Cassava Development Strategy
GDP	gross domestic product
GlobalGAP	Global Good Agricultural Practice
GNP	gross national product
HD	human development
HDI	Human Development Index
HIPC	Highly Indebted Poor Countries
HIV	human immunodeficiency virus
ICA	international commodity agreement
ICO	International Coffee Organization
IFAD	International Fund for Agricultural Development
IFPRI	International Food Policy Research Institute
ILO	International Labour Organization
IMF	International Monetary Fund
ITC	International Tin Council
IUF	International Union of Food, Agricultural, Hotel, Restaurant, Catering, Tobacco and Allied Workers' Associations

kg	kilogram
lb	pound (weight)
LDC	Least Developed Country
NEPAD	New Partnership for Africa's Development
ODI	Overseas Development Institute
OPEC	Organization of the Petroleum Exporting Countries
PPP	purchasing power parity
PRSP	Poverty Reduction Strategy Paper
SAP	structural adjustment programme
SDR	Special Drawing Right
SM	supply management
sq. km	square kilometre(s)
SSA	sub-Saharan Africa
TNC	transnational corporation
TRIMS	Trade-Related Investment Measures
TRIPS	Trade-Related Intellectual Property Rights
TVEs	township and village enterprises (in China)
UK	United Kingdom
UN	United Nations
UNCTAD	United Nations Conference on Trade and Development
UNDP	United Nations Development Programme
US	United States
Ush	Ugandan shilling
USSR	Union of Soviet Socialist Republics
WTO	World Trade Organization

Foreword: crisis year

Events move fast during a crisis, and so it has been since this book was written in the middle months of 2007. When I started writing it, loan-financed 'private equity' funds were busily buying up famous companies while speculative 'hedge funds' were well-established investors, among other things, in primary commodities, including foodstuffs such as maize (corn), wheat and rice. Indeed, we were told that a commodities 'supercycle' had placed the prices of foods, metals and other commodities on a long-term rising trend, which might even banish the boom-and-bust character for which their markets have always been renowned.

Then suddenly, in the usually quiet holiday month of August, the credit markets suffered what a leading banker called a 'heart attack'. Financiers lost confidence in the new debt instruments which lay behind the boom, the banks stopped lending to each other, and the financial authorities were left scratching their heads, since the methods they had applied to previous financial crises would not work on this one.

The world of high finance might seem a long way from the struggle for survival of smallholders, pastoral herders, rural labourers and their families in Ethiopia, Mongolia, Moldova, the Solomon Islands, Haiti and other poor countries, about whose plight this book is written. But in the world of global free markets which has developed since the 1980s, they are closely linked. Poor countries have been required by financial institutions to set their future on exports, which in most cases means primary commodities and more often than not the produce of their fields, trees and animals. The prices they receive for them are set in global markets and by corporations which order the produce and sell it on to the world's consumers.

These countries were advised to forget traditional concepts of food security, according to which they should ensure that their people will be fed without the need for supplies from abroad. Many abandoned food reserves which they had maintained as a safeguard against natural disaster and economic adversity. They were assured that, as long as export revenues were sufficient, food could always be bought on international markets.

If only life – and the world economy – were that simple. This book examines the policies of freeing up world markets, which have led to such unfathomable wealth for those who have worked in finance over the past 20 years. It describes the 'export orientation' trap in which poor countries have meanwhile been locked. We seem to have forgotten the lessons of the 1929 Wall Street crash, which discredited the similar *laissez-faire* policies of its day. A reliance on unfettered market forces has once again aggravated the poverty of many of the poorest and most vulnerable people on our planet. Few foresaw how much worse the trap would become in a few short months after the credit crisis began. When the financial markets weakened, investors moved much of their money into the markets for oil, gold, cereals and other commodities. That goes a long way towards explaining what transformed a food price problem in 2007 into the world food crisis of 2008.

Higher food prices should be welcomed if they increase the incomes of poor farmers. That takes some time, however, and it can only be assured with the aid of major reforms to the markets. Most developing countries are now caught in a vice: always dependent on unstable commodity markets for much of their export income, now they depend on the same for imports too, including basic foods. A generation ago they imported little or no food. The book explains why and how these changes in their trade came about, how the global markets and supply chains work, and how poor countries and their citizens can be released from the vice's grip. It suggests some ways in which a more civilized view of economics might be re-established. The first concern should be not to liberate trade and elevate high finance, but to let one billion poor people be sure of having secure roofs over their heads and enough food to stop them going to sleep hungry at night. It is to those people that this book is dedicated.

It could not have been written without the help and advice of dozens of other people over the past 30 years or more. It would be impossible to name them all. However, my thanks must go to the staff at Zed Books, who gave me every encouragement; especially to Tamsine O'Riordan, Susannah Trefgarne and the anonymous reviewers who read my book proposal. I would also like to thank a few other people for their help with my work over the last few years. Listed alphabetically, they are: Samuel Asfaha, Oli Brown, Anne-Claire Chambron, Hélène Delorme, Dominic Eagleton, Maveen Pereira, Sophie Powell, Alistair Smith and Bill Vorley. My apologies to anyone I have omitted. Some – including colleagues at the Common Fund for Commodities and UNCTAD – have graciously given me opportunities to investigate these questions even if they did not always agree with my conclusions. However, any faults in this book are entirely my own responsibility.

Thomas Lines • Brighton, May 2008

Introduction

Several hundred million of the world's poorest and most vulnerable people risk ending up soon on the economic scrapheap. If present policies continue, this risk will exist across much of the developing world and in some countries that until recently were regarded as developed and industrial. It may seem a bold claim until one examines the nature of modern poverty and the commercial and political forces which perpetuate it and are deepening the global economic divide. Discovery of the scale of poverty, and the inequalities which accompany it, can astonish even those in the rich world whose stock-in-trade is the plight of poor countries. Besides climate change, this is surely the most pressing problem facing our world today.

This book investigates how global policies have come to threaten national economies and, through them, the survival of hundreds of millions of poor rural people and their ways of life. Under globalization, poor countries, and the poorest people in other countries, have been marginalized. In my experience this is intuitively understood as a fact of modern life by people who come from such places. Similar concerns gave rise to the Make Poverty History campaign run by several British charities in recent years. They chose a powerful slogan which mobilized thousands of people and increased awareness of world poverty. However, several big questions remain unanswered in the public debate: What has actually made poverty? Why are poor people poor? Before poverty can become 'history', we need to know the answers to these questions. We must understand what (and where) the greatest poverty is, and examine global economic arrangements to see why poverty endures under them.

As a contribution to that task, this book examines how international trade in particular affects rural people and their livelihoods, what happens to the prices of poor countries' exports, and how the trade in them operates. This trade has fundamental inadequacies, which prejudice the chances of many poor people. In the present day we hear little about this as a major concern; this book draws fresh attention to the issue, with a view to overcoming the obstacles it lays in the path.

A central problem

As long ago as 1969 the Pearson Report on International Development, commissioned by the World Bank, described the widening gap between the developed and developing countries as 'a central problem of our times'.[1] More recently, the UN Development Programme (UNDP) argued that global inequalities in incomes and living standards had reached 'grotesque proportions'. It pointed out that the gap in national income per person (GNP *per capita*) between the countries with the richest fifth of the world's people and those with the poorest fifth had widened from 30:1 in 1960 to 60:1 in 1990 and 74:1 in 1995.[2] No doubt the gap is now wider still. Even more recently, the UNDP estimated that the world's 500 richest people shared an annual income of more than $100 billion, which was more than the combined incomes of the poorest 416 million.[3]

At the time of the Pearson Report, income gaps were actually narrowing. Within nations, income inequality is reported to have fallen between 1950 and the mid-1970s in 48 out of 73 countries surveyed.[4] And while the ratio in gross domestic product (GDP) *per capita*[5] between the richest and poorest regions of the world widened from 15:1 in 1950 to 19:1 in 1998, in 1973 it was narrower than in either of those years at 13:1.[6] But since 1973 Africa has displaced Asia (excluding Japan) as the poorest region. This book explores why African countries (and those with similar characteristics elsewhere, including parts of Asia) have experienced such stagnation, and what can be done about it now.

For most of the time since civilization began, people around the world have enjoyed broadly similar standards of living. It has been observed that, 'Nothing remotely like the income differences of our current world ... existed in 1800 or at any earlier time. Such inequality is a product of the industrial revolution.'[7] When European powers started to dominate the world in the imperial era, people almost everywhere were rather poor by modern standards, and the Europeans achieved their domination more as a consequence of military than of economic pre-eminence. According to one estimate, in 1820 the GDP *per capita* of Western Europe (already the richest part of the world at the time) was no more than three times that of Africa (the poorest then too).[8]

The sharp widening of income gaps since the Industrial Revolution indicates how unevenly the fruits of industry have been distributed. Severe inequality, a famous phenomenon in Victorian England, has persisted throughout the last two centuries. In recent years, there has been much talk of reducing poverty but not of reducing inequality or the gap in incomes. But surely inequality matters in itself. In the present world, someone born in the UK can expect to live more than twice as long as those in many other countries; how can anyone feel content with such arbitrary differences? If in 1969 the income gap was 'a central problem of our times', its present size indeed appears 'grotesque' and reducing it deserves even greater attention than it did nearly 40 years ago. It is hardly an original thought that a wide gap between the rich and the poor is characteristic of capitalism, but with all our present knowledge, it must surely be possible to again narrow that gap.

Outline of the book

Chapter 1 investigates who the poorest people in the world are, finding that most of them live in rural areas, scattered throughout much of the developing world. The book then seeks to explain the present crisis in rural incomes and propose some solutions to it. This chapter goes on to offer a series of economic reasons why certain countries have fallen behind in the 20 years of globalization.

Chapter 2 illustrates the historical background in previous centuries and sets out the recent international policies that have provoked the current situation. Chapter 3 examines the international commodity markets in particular and their role in defining poor countries' trade, and discusses the inefficiencies and failures of these markets. Chapter 4 examines another source of problems with agricultural prices: the growth of corporate power among supermarkets and other firms at the consumer end of supply chains. Chapter 5 stands back and argues for a different approach to development in general, to enable poorer countries to concentrate on developing their own economies and trade with neighbours at a similar level of development rather than putting all the emphasis on supplying global markets. This is especially relevant to Africa. Finally, Chapter 6 contains a summary of policy proposals.

Notes

1 Pearson (1969), p. 3. The Commission on International Development was led by Lester Pearson, a former prime minister of Canada.
2 UNDP (1999), pp. 104–5. National income per person (GNP *per capita*) refers to a country's gross national product divided by the number of inhabitants in the country; its aim is to give an idea how countries' incomes compare, irrespective of their population.
3 'On the (conservative) assumption that the world's 500 richest people listed by *Forbes* magazine have an income equivalent to no more than 5 per cent of their assets, their income exceeds that of the poorest 416 million people.' UNDP (2005), p. 37.
4 Kaplinsky (2005), p. 41.
5 Gross domestic product is, like GNP, a measure of the total monetary income accruing to a country over the course of a year. It is identical to the value of everything produced in that country. GDP measures only the value of things produced within the country while GNP also takes into account income received from nationally owned entities abroad (such as profits from the foreign subsidiaries of domestic companies) and payments of a similar sort made to other countries.
6 Solimano (2001), p. 12, Table 1, citing Maddison (2001), Tables B-10 and B-18 (pp. 241–61).
7 Lucas (2004).
8 Solimano (2001), as above. The topic is also discussed in Alam (2006).

1

Those who have fallen behind

It has been reported that the number of people living in absolute poverty is falling, and that the fight against poverty is therefore being won. This is at best a half-truth since it derives from the situation in two huge and quite atypical countries, India and China; even in those countries, poverty now appears to have been reduced far less than was previously thought, as we shall see at the end of this chapter. At the same time, many other developing countries have gone through a long period of economic stagnation or decline, and the rapid growth of urban economies in China, India and a few other countries must not be allowed to hide this bleak record. The lessons that other developing countries can draw directly from their economic success are limited.

This chapter will look at the facts of the case, first examining the question of what poverty is – not always as obvious as it might appear – and which groups of people are most affected by it, and then comparing data on the richest and poorest countries. After that, it will explain what economic characteristics are shared by the nations and people that have failed to benefit from globalization. The chapter concludes that there is a crisis facing rural economies worldwide; and the rest of this book will examine how that crisis affects those most vulnerable to it and what can be done to overcome it.

Just who is poor?

As the first task in our analysis, it is necessary to see just who are the poorest people, where in the world they live and how they derive their meagre livelihoods. Until recently, the common image of poverty in developing countries, as seen from the rich world, was of urban slums. As seen from many of the poor world's ministries, it often remains so: poor rural people are out of sight and therefore out of mind, just like their equivalents in many developed countries. Poverty in urban areas can be real and painful enough; but the overwhelming majority of the very poorest people are actually rural. A good guide to this is the *Rural Poverty Report*, published by the International Fund for Agricultural Development (IFAD) in 2001 and the most comprehensive survey there has been of rural poverty. According to it, three-quarters of the 1.2 billion people then living on less than US$1 a day lived and worked in rural areas.[1]

Poor people's circumstances vary greatly, but several common factors can be found. According to IFAD, the poorest of the rural poor generally live in remote areas, with 634 million of them in marginal lands (of whom 375 million are in Asia). In Latin America poverty is highest in some of the more remote, less densely populated areas, and many of the poorest regions are at high altitudes or have low levels of rainfall. There are also poor smallholders in dryland areas in West and Central Africa, Asia and the Pacific, Latin America and the Caribbean. Poor farmers in East and Southern Africa may be found in areas of low agricultural potential as well as areas of moderate to high agricultural potential, which is often unrealized.[2] Another author wrote that poor rural people

> are isolated in every sense. They have meagre holdings or access to land, little or no capital and few opportunities for off-farm employment. Labour demand is often insecure and seasonal. Extension services [offering agricultural advice] are few and far between, and research aimed specifically at their needs is sparse.[3]

The people described in these sources include large numbers of subsistence and near-subsistence farmers, who grow all the food that their households eat, or only purchase a limited amount in exchange for produce that they sell. Such people earn little monetary income, but they are not *necessarily* worse off than those who grow no food for themselves. However, it is estimated that about half of the world's *hungry* people are from smallholder farming communities (including subsistence farmers), while another 20 per cent are rural landless and about 10 per cent live in communities whose livelihoods depend on herding, fishing or forest resources; a very large proportion of the latter will also live at subsistence levels. The remaining 20 per cent of hungry people live in towns and cities.[4] So hunger, like low incomes, is concentrated in rural areas and much of it lies outside the monetary economy.

Indeed, poverty is a complex and elusive concept, and specialists differ as to whether it mainly concerns monetary incomes or less tangible factors such as marginalization, vulnerability, insecurity and dependence on other people. This is IFAD's rather ambiguous summary:

> Poverty has both physical and psychological dimensions. Poor people themselves strongly emphasize violence and crime, discrimination, insecurity and political repression, biased or brutal policing, and victimization by rude, neglectful or corrupt public agencies. . . . Some may feel poor or be regarded as poor if they cannot afford the sorts of things available to other people in their community. . . . [P]oor people report their condition largely in terms of material deprivation: not enough money, employment, food, clothing and housing, combined with inadequate access to health services and clean water; but they are also liable to give weight to such non-material factors as security, peace and power over decisions affecting their lives.[5]

Correspondingly, there is no consensus on how poverty should be measured. The most common measures are of the numbers or percentages of people living on less than US$1 or US$2 per day.[6] This measure may be crude but it is used by many international agencies and its clarity and simplicity lend it an obvious virtue. Other definitions are based on the numbers of people who are hungry or malnourished. However, all of these measurements can be disputed: there are various ways of defining hunger and malnutrition, while estimates of the number of people living on less than $1 a day have ranged from 353 million to 1.64 billion.[7]

As an example of these problems, John Sender has pointed out that most information on rural poverty comes from sample surveys, which are often based on official registers and therefore exclude numerous categories of people, such as workers living in temporary accommodation on construction sites or farms, squatters, and those who are in illegal housing, sleeping rough or engaged in the sexual services industry. In such surveys, he wrote, the poorest people will be under-represented.[8] However, the poorest households also frequently depend on women who perform manual agricultural wage labour.[9] This narrows the field to the 450 million or so waged agricultural workers around the world[10] and, more specifically among them, those women in poor countries who are in the most unskilled, precarious and irregular employment.

According to one author who knows about combating poverty in Bangladesh, 'The poorest are not just poorer than the poor. Extreme poverty is not a continuum of deprivation but a structural break.'[11] Another author, Xavier Godinot,[12] says that there is a close link between extreme poverty and the breakdown in an individual's relationship with their community. Godinot calls this social exclusion, but a more old-fashioned word might be destitution. It can reduce the chances of finding work and shelter, and it is what links poor people in the poorest countries with those who are poor, by local standards, in rich countries, even if their material standards and incomes are very different. As we shall see, a similar distinction can be made between developing countries in general and the very poorest group of them.

Poor people are vulnerable to risk. Farmers and agricultural workers face many kinds of risk to their livelihoods. Among these can be sudden price falls, an unexpected drop in the harvest, natural disasters, incidental events such as higher transport costs, the destruction of roads or other infrastructure, civil unrest or war, as well as illness, epidemics and other health hazards, and the death of a breadwinner. Low incomes and sudden, unexpected changes in income can expose people to food shortages and deprive them of basic health services and their children of education. Insufficient family income, indeed, is the main reason why children are sometimes pressed into labour.

People's responses to risk and vulnerability must be taken into account in the approach to fighting poverty. The World Bank has argued that poor farmers will often specialize in activities in which both risks and economic returns are low, even though it says this makes it hard for them to escape from poverty. For example, in Tanzania those farmers who have no livestock are more inclined to grow sweet potatoes (a low-risk, low-return crop) than farmers who do own livestock.[13] It should hardly be necessary to spell out why such caution prevails: a poor farmer or landless labourer will not willingly undertake any activity that incurs a risk of losing whatever little they actually have. It is important not to scorn such behaviour, for example by representing sweet potatoes and other root crops as in some way inferior. Such crops, including cassava, and some cereals such as sorghum and millet, can be important for food security, especially in parts of Africa where they will grow on thin soils and resist drought better than other staple crops do. Rather than suggesting that these low-risk crops are to be avoided, a sensible approach to reducing poverty would accept that they are what many poor people grow, with good reason, and build on that. I shall have more to say on this in Chapter 5, in particular when I discuss a successful programme of cassava promotion that the World Bank has been criticized for ignoring.

There are broadly three kinds of agricultural activity in developing countries: large farms and plantations, which employ many workers; small farms (of a few acres or hectares at most), which are generally based on the household and family but may employ a handful of workers, at least at peak times such as the harvest; and people who have no land and earn a living from working on large or small farms or in non-agricultural occupations. There are many crossovers between these categories; for example, members of smallholding households often work on other people's farms or outside agriculture, at least at certain times of the year. But these categories are useful in helping us to organize our thoughts.

However, there are problems in defining which countries are the poorest. Development institutions classify them in three main ways. The World Bank divides all countries into three income categories, according to their GDP *per capita*, expressed in US dollars: high-, middle- and low-income, the middle-income category being further divided between 'upper middle-income' and 'lower middle-income'. In 2004 there were 59 countries in the low-income category. This

Table 1 The countries with the highest human development indicators

Country and its UNDP human development ranking, 2004	Population in millions, 2004	Landlocked	GDP per capita, US$ (PPP)		Year of highest value	Primary goods exports as % of merchandise exports, 2004
			2004	Highest during 1975–2004		
1 Norway	4.6		38,454	38,454	2004	77
2 Iceland	0.3		33,051	33,051	2004	82
3 Australia	19.9		30,331	30,747	1997	58
4 Ireland	4.1		38,827	38,827	2004	10
5 Sweden	9.0		29,541	29,541	2004	14
6 Canada	32.0		31,263	31,263	2004	35
7 Japan	127.9		29,251	29,251	2004	3
8 USA	295.4		39,676	39,676	2004	14
9 Switzerland	7.2	Yes	33,040	34,304	2002	7
10 Netherlands	16.2		31,789	31,889	2002	30
11 Finland	5.2		29,951	29,951	2004	16
12 Luxembourg	0.5	Yes	69,961	69,961	2004	13
13 Belgium	10.4		31,096	31,096	2004	18
14 Austria	8.2	Yes	32,276	32,276	2004	15
15 Denmark	5.4		31,914	31,914	2004	31
16 France	60.3		29,300	29,300	2004	17
17 Italy	58.0		28,180	28,180	2004	11
18 UK	59.5		30,821	30,821	2004	18
19 Spain	42.6		25,047	25,047	2004	21
20 New Zealand	4.0		23,413	23,413	2004	65
21 Germany	82.6		28,303	28,303	2004	9
22 Hong Kong, China	7.0		30,822	30,822	2004	3

23 Israel	6.6		24,382	25,959	2000	5
24 Greece	11.1		22,205	22,205	2004	38
25 Singapore	4.3		28,077	28,077	2004	13
26 South Korea	47.6		20,499	20,499	2004	8
27 Slovenia	2.0		20,939	20,939	2004	10
28 Portugal	10.4		19,629	20,117	2001	15
29 Cyprus	0.8		22,805	22,805	2004	35
30 Czech Republic	10.2	Yes	19,408	19,408	2004	10
High HD — total	1,275.0		26,568	—	—	17

Sources: UNDP, European Commission, FAO, Oxfam America, UN Economic Commission for Africa, World Bank.

Table 2 The countries defined as of low human development

Country and its UNDP human development ranking, 2004	Population in millions, 2004	Global hunger index, 2007*	Landlocked	GDP per capita, US$ (PPP)			Commodity-dependent in 2003–5†	Primary exports as % of merchandise exports, 2004
				2004	Highest during 1975–2004	Year of highest value		
147 Togo	6.0	20.4		1,536	2,218	1980	Yes	53
148 Djibouti	0.8	17.1		1,993	2,413	1995	N.A.	–
149 Lesotho	1.8	13.2	Yes	2,619	2,619	2004	No	–
150 Yemen	20.3	31.5		879	879	2004	No	97
151 Zimbabwe	12.9	24.8	Yes	2,065	3,224	1998	Yes	72
152 Kenya	33.5	21.0		1,140	1,247	1990	Yes	79
153 Mauritania	3.0	18.1		1,940	1,967	2001	N.A.	–
154 Haiti	8.4	27.0		1,892	3,423	1980	N.A.	–
155 Gambia	1.5	18.8		1,991	2,137	1986	No	73 (2003)
156 Senegal	11.4	18.0		1,713	1,725	1976	No	61
157 Eritrea	4.2	40.3		977	1,246	1997	Yes	–
158 Rwanda	8.9	26.3	Yes	1,263	1,451	1983	Yes	90 (2003)
159 Nigeria	128.7	19.1		1,154	1,154	2004	No	98 (2003)
160 Guinea	9.2	21.8		2,180	2,197	2002	Yes	75 (2002)
161 Angola	15.5	31.5		2,180	2,764	1992	N.A.	–
162 Tanzania	37.6	26.1		674	674	2004	Yes	80
163 Benin	8.2	17.4		1,091	1,099	2003	Yes	91 (2002)
164 Côte d'Ivoire	17.9	17.4		1,551	2,977	1978	Yes	78 (2003)
165 Zambia	11.5	31.1	Yes	943	1,557	1976	No	90
166 Malawi	12.6	24.5	Yes	646	733	1979	Yes	84

167 DR Congo	55.9		705	2,469	1975	N.A.	–
168 Mozambique	19.4		1,237	1,237	2004	Yes	96 (2002)
169 Burundi	7.3	Yes	677	933	1991	Yes	95
170 Ethiopia	75.6	Yes	756	776	1983	Yes	89 (2003)
171 Chad	9.4	Yes	2,090	2,090	2004	N.A.	–
172 Central Afr. Rep.	4.0	Yes	1,094	1,761	1977	Yes	63 (2003)
173 Guinea-Bissau	1.5		722	1,106	1997	N.A.	–
174 Burkina Faso	12.8	Yes	1,169	1,169	2004	Yes	92
175 Mali	13.1	Yes	998	998	2004	Yes	–
176 Sierra Leone	5.3		561	1,151	1982	Yes	–
177 Niger	13.5	Yes	779	1,322	1979	Yes	91 (2003)
Low HD – total	571.7		1,113	–	–	–	71

* A figure of more than 10 on the Intenational Food Policy Research Institute's Global Hunger Index is defined as 'serious', more than 20 as 'alarming' and more than 30 as 'extremely alarming'. The index is based on three indicators: the undernourished as a percentage of the population; the prevalence of underweight in children under five years old; and the under-five mortality rate. See Deutscher Welthungerhilfe et al. (2007).

† Based on Gibbon (2007), which only covers countries that report to the UN's Comtrade system. Others are marked here 'N.A.' (not applicable). Gibbon's definition of commodity dependency is quoted in Chapter 3, note 18.

Sources: UNDP, European Commission, FAO, Gibbon (2007), IFPRI, Oxfam America, UN Economic Commission for Africa, World Bank.

classification is relatively easy to measure but subject to the same criticism of over-simplicity as a monetary definition of personal poverty. So two other classifications, originated at the United Nations, use greater numbers of indicators. The UN Development Programme classifies countries as of 'high', 'medium' and 'low' human development (HD) according to their people's average life expectancy at birth and standards of education in addition to GDP *per capita* (which itself is adjusted for the local cost of living). In the latest year for which the UNDP gives figures (2004), there were 31 countries in the low-HD category. Finally, a still more complex set of development indicators is used to define the Least Developed Countries (LDCs), of which there are now 50 (compared with just 24 when the UN introduced the category in 1971). This book makes use of the Human Development Index (HDI) and LDC categories: the former for its simplicity and accessibility (the figures are updated every year and available in the annual *Human Development Report* on the UNDP's website); and LDCs at times for the greater sophistication of the concept.

Not keeping pace

According to their advocates, global free markets enable total wealth to increase, creating a rising tide that will bring up the livelihoods of all the world's people. And indeed, in recent times the richest countries have all enjoyed sustained economic growth and prosperity. As can be seen in Table 1, GDP *per capita*, on a purchasing power parity (PPP) basis, reached its highest-ever level in 2004 (the latest year shown) in all but two of the 30 countries with the highest human development indicators. Traditionally reliant on industry, these countries' economies are increasingly dominated by finance and other services and the so-called 'knowledge economy'. This means the command of research and development as well as the ownership of international brands, patents, copyrights and other forms of 'intellectual property', which enable the countries' corporations to exert international economic control via the command of worldwide supply chains.

The evidence of their sustained economic success is likely to surprise few people. However, even to those given to pessimism about world poverty, the pattern at the other end of the scale can come as quite a shock. A large group of countries has continuously failed to share in economic advance. Table 2 shows that real GDP *per capita* reached its peak in 2004 in only eight of the 31 countries defined as of low human development, while twelve of them remained *poorer than they were before 1985*. That was before the international policies of structural adjustment and trade liberalization took hold; we will consider these in Chapter 2. In three countries (the Democratic Republic of the Congo, Senegal and Zambia) the most prosperous year was more than 30 years ago – either the very first or the second year in the UNDP's series. The Congo's real income per person is estimated to have fallen by 71 per cent over the 29 years from 1975 to 2004.[14]

Putting these figures together, we find that in 2004 the countries with high human development had some 67 *times* the average dollar income per person of those at the bottom: their GDP *per capita* was US$26,999, while that of countries with low HD was just $402.[15] Even when the figures are adjusted for differences in purchasing power (as they are in Tables 1 and 2), the high-HD countries remained some 24 times as well off. And this is not a contrast of the extremes: there are 63 countries with high HD and they count between them 20 per cent of the world's people; while 31 countries are of low HD, with 9 per cent of the world's population.

The latter countries rely on the production and export of primary commodities – agriculture and minerals – to make their way in the world, and that will form much of the subject matter of this book. Wealth in the modern world evidently derives from manufactures and services, and perhaps the *control* of commodity supplies, but not from the production of most commodities themselves. The progressive diversification of economic activity, moving from the primary sector (food and raw materials) into the industrial and service sectors, almost amounts to a definition of economic development as traditionally understood. This is the bridge that China and India are crossing as they develop the production of manufactured goods and some globally traded services (such as call centres and financial businesses' 'back offices').

This stark contrast between the richest and poorest countries creates a problem for the process of development itself. For it is accompanied by a huge gap not only in purchasing power and technological capability but in the understanding that people have of what are 'normal' standards, even in apparently simple matters such as food. As a result of the rapid increase in their means, rich countries' citizens have become very demanding about their food and other purchases; but it is often very onerous for farmers in *developed* countries to meet those requirements, let alone those in the developing world. We will examine this question in Chapter 4.

Poverty under globalization

It could be said that the set of problems discussed in this book is typically African. The biggest geographical concentration of poverty is in Africa and every one of the 23 countries with the lowest human development is on that continent.[16] However, it is not our task to look for specifically 'African' explanations.[17] Many people try to do that but, in my view, doing so only obscures deeper issues. After all, there is severe poverty on every continent. In a similar list to the UNDP's but on the basis of GDP *per capita* alone, the 30 most disadvantaged countries would come from a wider geographical range than do the 30 lowest on the HDI. They would include East Timor and Kyrgyzstan (if GDP was measured in unadjusted US dollars), or Moldova and the Solomon Islands (if the valuations were adjusted for PPP). That spreads the net across five continents, including Europe.

Is it then possible to identify any economic or geographical characteristics which the poorest countries have in common, irrespective of their continent? Indeed it is: four distinguishing features are generally found in the countries that have fallen behind during the 20 years of globalization. Let us see what they are.

Small population
Many African countries have quite small populations, as do all four of the countries named above on other continents with low incomes *per capita* (East Timor, Kyrgyzstan, Moldova and the Solomon Islands).

Indeed, the total population of the 53 states in Africa, at around 880 million people, is substantially less than either China or India alone, with national populations of 1.3 billion and 1.1 billion respectively. The 31 low-HD countries have a combined population of 572 million, or an average of 18.4 million each: roughly half the average of all countries in the world. They therefore lack large internal markets and cannot exploit economies of scale, a vital economic fact that sets them apart from vast, populous China and India. Even in the past, India and China grew faster than other countries, although they pursued 'closed' economic policies that are conventionally dismissed today as prejudicial to development. Over the period 1965–85, income *per capita* in China and India grew at 3.5 per cent per year while such growth in other low-income countries was at less than 0.5 per cent. In both countries, the fruits of that growth also spread more widely through the population than has their very fast growth of recent years. Over the same 20-year period, income growth per person in lower-middle-income countries was at 2.6 per cent; even among upper-middle-income developing countries, it was no more than 3.3 per cent per year.[18]

Moreover, in both China and India, industry was well implanted before economic liberalization began (which was in the late 1970s and the early 1990s respectively). The origin of India's largest corporation, Tata, goes some way back: in colonial times Jamsetji Tata established a cotton mill in 1869, and the firm opened a steel mill at Jamshedpur in Bihar in 1907. As is well known, many technologies were invented in China earlier than in Europe, and in the modern period a wave of industrialization took place there under Soviet tutelage in the 1950s, followed by a vogue for rural factories before Mao Zedong's death in 1976. This puts those two countries in a very different position from smaller neighbours, such as Laos and Nepal, and other small countries in Africa and elsewhere. Besides industry, large size permitted them to develop a greater number and complexity of services funded by the state, such as higher education and research. Small countries, on the other hand, are more vulnerable to external economic shocks, partly because of the greater dependence on foreign trade that they usually have.[19]

Even among today's poorest countries, the larger ones have tended to be the better economic performers. Not only have India and China gradually risen out of the lowest categories of income and development, but Bangladesh, the largest LDC with some 140 million people, has had one of the highest economic growth rates *per capita* over the last 20 years, and has rapidly diversified its exports away from its former narrow commodities base. The greater size of its home market permits greater diversity and differentiation of output for local firms, facilitating the generation of investment surpluses for further development, just as in its two giant neighbours.

Remoteness from world markets

A second great disadvantage is geographical remoteness, mainly that of countries landlocked in the middle of a continent (as many in Africa are) and small island states. It is no coincidence that all the successful East Asian countries have direct access to coasts and major shipping routes: for the smaller ones, the easier access to external markets was one factor that helped to counter the negative effects of small size.[20] Likewise, industry has boomed in the coastal provinces of China but its inland provinces lag a long way behind.

Of the 31 countries of low human development, 12 are landlocked (and 9 of the 13 that have the very lowest HD scores), but only 4 of the 30 with the highest HD scores are. And it so happens that of the 31 developing countries that are landlocked, 15 are in Africa. Landlocked states elsewhere include Bolivia and Moldova (the poorest countries on their continents) and several Asian countries with very low *per capita* incomes, such as Kyrgyzstan, Laos, Mongolia, Nepal and Tajikistan. Other poor countries, such as the Solomon Islands, are maritime but remote; the only LDC in the Americas is a small island state (or rather, half an island): Haiti.[21]

Historically, much of this is a long-term consequence of the transfer several centuries ago of long-distance trade to the sea from former land routes, such as the Silk Road, which linked China with the Mediterranean Sea and Europe, and the Sahelian route via Timbuktu, which linked the Mediterranean with West Africa's forest zone. This change arose from Europe's commercial expansion by sea, which started in Spain and Portugal in the fifteenth century. In earlier times the Silk Road's passage across arid Central Asia had enriched oasis towns like Bukhara and Samarkand, fomented the Sogdian and Seljuk empires, and then that of Emir Timur (Tamerlane) in Samarkand; while, before the time of slavery, the Sahel was home to several great states, including those from which modern Mali and Ghana take their names. It is a further misfortune that poverty is exacerbated today by climate change, which affects these remote continental regions as severely as anywhere, as seen for example in the drying up of the Aral Sea in Central Asia and Lake Chad in West Africa.

Remoteness matters because it increases the costs of trade. The problem is compounded if the main port or ports serving a country are small, since this pushes the unit costs of transport up further. Naturally, the ports serving poor countries tend to be small, due to their low volumes of trade. So location matters, for example having a sea coast, preferably on a major shipping route; as does size, due to economies of scale. A related factor is low density of population, which increases the costs of transport and distribution within a country. This is a feature of many African countries but not many in Asia, except in landlocked Central Asia, including Mongolia.

In recent times the importance of transport costs for trade has grown further, as tariffs have been reduced.[22] The unit costs of transport, port charges and so on are as important as actual distance. Between small and remote farms and an export port, there is likely to be a greater number of intermediaries than in the case of larger farms, and this further raises the export price or reduces the share of it received by the farmer and the agricultural worker. Poor roads and other transport links increase costs by making for slower and less efficient carriage. The recent increases in oil prices have added to the importance of these factors and further reduced the terms of trade of landlocked and small island states. These are among the numerous obstacles that prevent poor and remote countries, and their rural communities, from making good use of foreign trade.[23]

Dependence on commodity exports

In general, the poorest countries are the most dependent in their trade on exports of primary goods. In every one of the low-HD countries for which the UNDP showed this figure, primary goods accounted for more than half of merchandise exports in 2004. In nine of them 90 per cent or more of these exports were primary goods, peaking at 98 per cent in the case of Nigeria and 97 per cent in the Yemen. By contrast, the share of primary products is much lower at the top end of the HDI list, falling below 10 per cent of merchandise exports in Germany, Japan, South Korea and Switzerland.[24] Poor countries' incomes do not depend as exclusively on commodities as in the past, since substantial amounts now come in as remittances from their citizens working in other countries where wages are higher and from foreign aid and a certain number of services, such as tourism. However, most of these are make-do sources of income, which merely reveal the extent of a country's economic dependency; their greater relative weight is also a function of the long-term decline of commodity prices, which I discuss below.

Dependence on small numbers of primary products leaves a country vulnerable to the sharp changes to which the world markets for these products are prone and, in the case of agricultural commodities, to the adverse effects on production of the weather and natural disasters. A recent study identified 43 developing countries as dependent on commodity exports in 2003–5, to the extent that at least half of their merchandise exports by value were made up of commodities, other than oil.[25] Of the 20 countries with the lowest HDI indicators in 2004, 14 were among those 43 countries. Of the other six, one (Nigeria) is one of the 25 countries in the world that are most dependent on oil exports[26] and four others could not be classified because they did not appear in the database used by the author; one of these (Angola) is also one of the 25 most oil-dependent countries.[27]

Commodity prices have long been known to be volatile, but in the 1980s and 1990s they also fell sharply against the prices of manufactured goods and services. The recent boom in many markets may have reduced this trend but it has not eliminated it: between

1960 and 2005 the real prices of agricultural commodities fell by half.[28] This means that agrarian countries have to export twice the quantities of 1960 in order to purchase the same amount of manufactured imports. In September 2003 the UN Conference on Trade and Development (UNCTAD) invited a group that it called 'eminent persons' to discuss the issue, and they spelt out the macroeconomic impact: 'When principal petroleum and manufactured goods exporters are excluded, the terms of trade of developing countries have declined by more than 20 per cent since 1980. For African countries, which comprise the most commodity-dependent group, the decline is more than 25 per cent.'[29] This means that since 1980 the prices of Africa's exports had fallen by more than one-quarter in relation to its import prices (a change of ratio from 100:100 to less than 75:100). African countries must therefore increase the volume of their exports by *more than one-third* if they want again to import as much of other goods as they did then.

This problem used to be widely understood, and there were some successful attempts to act on it between the 1950s and the 1970s. But it has been ignored since the 1980s as the prevailing orthodoxy emphasizes the virtues of unrestricted markets.

Rural poverty with food imports
We have already seen that most of the poorest people live in rural areas, and many of them are either subsistence or semi-subsistence farmers or landless labourers. We have also seen a historical association between economic development and the move away from an agrarian economy, but over recent decades it has been prejudiced by the decline in agricultural commodity prices. It is therefore no surprise to find that, in general, the countries that have fallen behind are predominantly agrarian, depending on agriculture and livestock for most of their production, employment and foreign trade. Some of them earn the greatest part of their export revenue from minerals, such as oil (in Angola and Nigeria) and alumina (in Mozambique), or, occasionally, services like tourism (in Eritrea) and even air transport (in Ethiopia).[30] But even in those countries, agriculture is the main source of productive activity, livelihoods and employment.

However, we saw in Table 2 the serious hunger status of these countries; and paradoxically, despite their agrarian character, they actually import food. The Food and Agriculture Organization of the UN (FAO) defines 82 countries as low-income food-deficit countries,[31] which means that they import food to a greater calorific value than the food they export. That is nearly half of all the states in the world, and they include all but one of the 31 countries with low HD indicators. By contrast, both India and China have been careful for several decades *not* to import more food than they export; on the other hand, there is a worrying parallel with the USSR's debilitating need for grain imports over many years before it collapsed. We shall look at this question more closely in Chapter 5.

The long-term fall in prices has reached the point where it undermines agriculture's profitability as a business,[32] in many cases even when prices have risen from the all-time lows of 2001–3. The lack of profitability makes it *more* difficult for small farmers to move out of poverty by selling crops for cash. Some leading experts in rural development see additional reasons why small-farm agriculture may no longer have the advantages that development thinkers used to assume it had. In one influential paper, eight such reasons were listed. They included the facts that many small farmers lack the skills required to manage new technologies; small farms pay more for agricultural inputs and receive less for their outputs than large farms do; and small farmers find it hard to satisfy the quality and timeliness required by new systems of commodity supply.[33]

The four features discussed above are characteristic of a great many African countries: together they amount to a clear indication of why poverty remains more widespread there than on other continents.[34] Niger, for example, which was at the bottom of the Human Development Index in 2006, displays all four features, and they formed the background to its food crisis in 2004–5. Niger's vast territory of 1.27 million sq. km reportedly contains deposits of oil, coal, iron ore, tin, phosphates, molybdenum, gypsum and salt, while the exploitation of gold began there recently.[35] Before the crisis, its monetary economy had expanded impressively, with GDP growth of

5.5 per cent in 2000 and 12.6 per cent in 2001. But, in spite of this, Niger's terms of trade were deteriorating. Its leading exports have been uranium (a chronically weak market) and livestock and vegetables (sold to neighbouring countries); with few roads, a topography that is mostly desert and semi-desert, and a long distance to the sea, the country's 11 million people are left to survive on the 3.5 per cent of its land that is arable, of which just 0.01 per cent is under permanent crops. The fact that Niger shares with Mali and Burkina Faso the world's lowest educational attainments is another handicap.[36]

But this is not just an African problem: the same four factors apply to Moldova, which after the break-up of the USSR quickly became the poorest country in Europe. It is small, landlocked between Romania and the Ukraine, and dependent on agriculture. Much of it has returned to small-scale subsistence farming since its former collective farms collapsed during the 1990s. Moldova experienced one of the sharpest falls in production and income on record, its GDP *per capita* on a PPP basis falling by 63 per cent from a peak in 1989 (shortly before the collapse of the USSR) until 2001;[37] there has been some recovery since then.

A global crisis

It is hard to escape the thought that in recent years the global system has failed poor people in rural areas everywhere. We share the basic analysis of Canada's National Farmers Union:

> To solve the farm income crisis, we must understand it. And to understand the crisis, we must never lose sight of three key facts:
> • The crisis is at least 20 years old;
> • It is global; and
> • It is unprecedented.[38]

The agricultural crisis is indeed global, and we must reassert this in the face of those who would pit farmers in the global South against those of the North. The North's agricultural subsidies frequently create unfair competition for developing countries, but it must not be forgotten that in recent years the average *Canadian* farm lost between C$10,000 and C$20,000 per year,[39] while English farm incomes (including subsidies) varied between £10,100 in 1999–2000 and £31,200 in 2003–4.[40] In nearly every year this was less than the national average wage, although English farms are sizeable businesses exploiting on average 55 hectares of land. Between 1988 and 2006 the prices received by British farmers for agricultural produce increased by only 3.4 per cent[41] although retail food prices increased by more than 50 per cent.[42] Thus the agricultural crisis of the 1990s and the first years of the twenty-first century has been worldwide, affecting farmers throughout the rich world and in rapidly expanding developing countries such as India and China, as well as those in the poorest countries, whose situation we have already described. And if present policies continue, the rural crisis may be only entering its most damaging phase, in which the concentration of agricultural supply and the economies of scale that it requires will displace millions upon millions of small farmers. This concentration is forced in part by the rapid worldwide spread of supermarkets and the supply chains that they control. This threat will be examined in Chapter 4.

In developing countries the agricultural crisis is more or less pervasive, affecting places as diverse as Brazil, India, Moldova, Nepal and the Philippines, besides all of Africa. It severely affects the most important exports of poor countries. And it was recently calculated that much more poverty remains even in India and China than had been thought. The Asian Development Bank has indicated that there are 300 million people in China living on less than $1 per day on a PPP basis, which is three times the previous estimate; and 800 million in India, which is twice the previous estimate. The data also suggest that the Chinese economy is 40 per cent smaller than was thought, when adjusted for differences in currency values by the PPP method.[43]

In India and China, the urban–rural divide has become a serious political problem. In India, it is widely accepted that the Bharatiya Janata Party lost the 2004 general election, in spite of rapid GDP growth, because of the sharp contrast between the party's rhetoric of 'India Shining' and the reality of deep agrarian crisis. After 13 years of economic liberalization, the general situation was described in these words:

The recent past has witnessed the slowest rate of employment growth in post-independence history, agrarian crisis and worsening food security for the poor across the country. There are daily reports of starvation deaths and increasing numbers of suicides by indebted farmers unable to cope with the strain. Small producers are being wiped out in many sectors. Traditional moneylenders, who had been marginalised by decades of efforts to bring institutional banking to the rural areas, are making a comeback, emboldened by the financial liberalisation measures that have undermined the spread of banking to the poor. The availability of public services and access to them have deteriorated for most people, especially – but not only – in the rural areas. The majority of India's citizens live in more fragile, vulnerable and insecure material circumstances than before.[44]

According to the National Health and Family Survey of 2005–6, 46.3 per cent of Indian children under the age of three were malnourished and nearly 80 per cent were anaemic – an improvement on 51 per cent of under-threes underweight in 1992–3, but in Madhya Pradesh, a poor rural state, the figures had worsened since the late 1990s.[45] The nutritional situation was spelt out like this, also in 2004:

> Between the early 1990s when economic reforms began, and at present, taking three-year averages, the annual absorption of foodgrains per head has come down from 177 kg to 155 kg. Such low absorption levels were last seen in the initial years of World War II... Over four-fifths of the total fall has taken place in the last five years alone... This steep and unprecedented fall in foodgrains absorption in the last five years has entailed a sharp increase in the numbers of people in hunger, particularly in rural areas, and for very many it has meant starvation.[46]

So, while the worldwide gap between the richest and poorest people has been widening, the evidence actually shows little sign of improvement in the absolute position of the poorest since the era of globalization started in the 1980s; quite the contrary. China too has experienced an extended wave of rural unrest, with protests over land confiscation, pollution, access to irrigation, public transport, corruption and other matters. Here too, the underlying cause is unequal access to the benefits of economic growth.[47] Related phenomena of social marginalization, urban drift and emigration are seen in many other countries that have not shared the two Asian giants' relative prosperity. Other severe problems, especially HIV/ Aids and climate change, reinforce these difficulties. It is a race against time to resolve the rural crisis while avoiding anything that would risk adding significantly to carbon emissions. But it is no solution to insist on more of the same – *more* market, *more* trade liberalization. The markets themselves have created a large part of the problem, as we shall see in chapters 3 and 4. And so indeed they always have done: that hard-learnt lesson has been dangerously ignored over the last 20 years.

Notes

1 IFAD (2001), pp. 1 and 20. IFAD defines as 'extreme consumption poverty' an income *per capita* of less than US$1 a day, on the basis of purchasing power parity (PPP). More information can be found at «www.ruralpovertyportal. org/english/topics/index.htm» (June 2007).

2 *Ibid.*, p. 21.

3 Conway (1997), pp. 134–5, quoted in Ashley and Maxwell (2001), pp. 397–8.

4 FAO (2004b), p. 25, citing the UN Millennium Project's Hunger Taskforce.

5 IFAD (2001), Box 2.3, p. 19.

6 With local prices converted into dollars at exchange rates that purport to even out price differences between countries, using the so-called 'purchasing power parity' method.

7 See Kaplinsky (2005), pp. 33–7.

8 Sender (2003), p. 414.

9 *Ibid.*, p. 413, citing Sender (2002).

10 The number of 450 million is provided by IUF, the food workers' international trade union secretariat. Their website is «www.iuf.org».

11 Matin (2005), p. 1. Imran Matin is the research director of the Bangladesh Rural Advancement Committee. For more information on BRAC, see «www.brac.net» and also UNDP (2005), Box 1.7 on p. 37 ('Bangladesh – moderate growth, rapid human development').

12 Godinot *et al.* (2005), p. 4.

13 World Bank (2001), pp. 142–3. This edition of the *World Development Report* was devoted to 'attacking poverty', and Part 4 in particular to issues of security, including the management of risk.

14 UNDP (2006), Table 14, pp. 331–4. It shows the DRC's estimated GDP *per capita* at PPP to have fallen from US$2,469 in 1975 to $705 in 2004. Senegal's GDP *per capita* at PPP in 2004 was just below the peak figure it reached in 1976, at $1,713 compared with $1,725, while Zambia was down 38 per cent at $943 compared with its 1976 peak of $1,557. In Madagascar (which is just above the 'low human development' category), the peak was reached in 1975, the first year of the HDI series, at $1,356. By 2004 it had fallen 37 per cent from there to $857. (All the PPP GDP figures are expressed at 2004 prices.)

15 *Ibid*.

16 The 24th and 28th lowest are Haiti and the Yemen respectively.

17 Issues that are specific to Africa are explored in UNCTAD (2003b).

18 ODI (1988), p. 6, citing World Bank.

19 See Guillaumont (2005), pp. 15–17.

20 See UNDP (2003), p. 74.

21 The United Nations recognizes 41 countries as small-island developing states. See FAO (2005).

22 Santiso (2005), p. 19.

23 See UNCTAD (2006a), Chapter 5, 'The infrastructure divide' (pp. 193– 220).

24 UNDP (2006), Table 16, pp. 339–42.

25 Gibbon (2007), p. 6. Gibbon's definition was based on the periods 1993–5 and 2003–5, but in this book I consider only the 43 countries which he found had matched his criteria in 2003–5.

26 Ross (2001), p. 7.

27 Gibbon's information was drawn from the UN's Comtrade database («comtrade.un.org/db»), which does not cover all countries. Among the 20 low-HD countries, only Zambia is then absent. Gibbon calculated Zambia's commodity exports to be only 42.7 per cent of all exports by value in 2003–5 (personal communication).

28 UNCTAD (2006b), Figure 1.A2, p. 20.

29 UNCTAD (2003d), Chap. II, Para. 32.

30 Data from UNCTAD (2005). This book specifies each LDC's main export sector in 2003, which is when the prices for tropical agricultural exports were at their lowest. The relative importance of export sectors is therefore partly a consequence of the decline in prices and revenues of agricultural products.

31 The 82 countries are listed by the FAO at «www.fao.org/countryprofiles/lifdc.asp?lang=en».

32 As argued by Ashley and Maxwell (2001), pp. 403–4.

33 *Ibid.*, p. 407.

34 In another recent book – see Collier (2007) – 58 poor countries were identified as facing one or more of four 'poverty traps', although these were

defined quite differently from my list. Its author divided the world's people into three groups: a billion or so living in rich countries; four billion in countries in the middle, many of which are experiencing fast economic growth; and the 'bottom billion' in the 58 countries just mentioned. That is not unlike this book's analysis; but Collier's emphasis was on the differences between the bottom billion and the four billion in the middle. However, it seems to me that explanations of the plight of the 'bottom billion' can be found in their relationship with the wealthy power brokers at the top.

35   Issa (2005).

36   UNDP (2004), Table 11, p. 179.

37   UNDP (2003), Table 12, p. 280.

38   National Farmers Union (2005), p. 2.

39   *Ibid.*, p. 3.

40   Expressed in 2005–6 prices; National Statistics (2006). English farm incomes were higher in 2007 thanks to increases in cereal and milk prices.

41   DEFRA (2007a).

42   DEFRA (2007b). I am grateful to Peter Kendall and Carmen Suarez at the UK's National Farmers Union for drawing my attention to the last two pieces of data.

43   See Keidel (2007) and ADB (2007).

44   Ghosh (2004).

45   Yee (2007).

46   Patnaik (2004), p. 1.

47   See, for example, *BBC News 24*, 12 March 2007, «news.bbc.co.uk/1/hi/world/asia-pacific/6441295.stm»; *The Guardian*, 14 April 2006, «www.guardian.co.uk/china/ story/0,,1753843,00.html»; *Washington Post*, 28 January 2006, «www.washingtonpost.com/wp-dyn/content/article/2006/01/27/AR2006012701588.html»; and *BBC News 24*, 20 January 2006, «news.bbc.co.uk/1/hi/world/asia-pacific/4630820.stm» (all of them viewed in June 2007).

2
How poverty is made

Why has such deep poverty persisted when rich countries have prospered so much? What policies were responsible and how should they be changed? Today's conventional wisdom holds that if markets are allowed to work without hindrance, they will lift all people out of poverty. But this was found to be a fallacy at much earlier stages in the history of capitalism, and was said to have been long discredited when I was introduced to economics in the late 1960s. And there is strong evidence that the rural crisis has arisen largely *as a result of* world markets being freed up, with inevitable consequences for countries that are in a weak position to benefit from this process. Is the insistence on free markets that now predominates – as it did in Europe's imperial heyday 100 years ago – necessarily better than the managed markets that prevailed in the decades after the Second World War? Prevailing ideas in economics do change from one generation to another and, like most things human, they are partly governed by fashion. Surely what matters is not the intellectual fashion of the day but what can be deduced from the evidence.

This chapter will relate the background to the poor countries' rural crisis, first in terms of their histories and then with an extended account of the policies of the last 25 years. It will first review the history of global trade and imperialism since the first European ocean voyages were made in the fifteenth century. This will be followed by an account of the change of policy which was led by the World Bank in the 1980s, and its implications for the trading position of the countries subjected to it. Two more sections will consider the political stance of the state that is required for successful development, in the light of recent experience. Finally, the chapter will review the overall outcomes of the last 20 years' international policies.

What made countries poor?

Rich and poor countries differ in what things they produce, how diverse those things are, what prices they are sold for, and what each country manages to sell abroad. A poor country has a narrower economic base than a rich one, and depends mostly on primary commodities for its merchandise exports – foods and agricultural or mineral raw materials. On the other hand, 'advanced' or 'developed' countries also produce 'secondary' (manufactured) goods and a wide range of services (sometimes called 'tertiary' products). These provide them with larger amounts of capital to invest in future economic advance.

The economies of most of today's poor countries were forged in the colonial era to serve European imperial centres. The former countries supplied the metropolises with raw materials and exotic foodstuffs, and provided markets for their processed and manufactured goods. When Europe's maritime expansion started at the end of the continent's Middle Ages, its adventurers and traders went in search of spices and luxuries such as fine cloths from the East, and gold and silver from America. They brought home agricultural products which they discovered in those regions, such as cocoa, maize, tobacco and potatoes. They then started the overseas *cultivation* for European consumption of tropical crops like coffee, cocoa, sugar cane and tea. The slave trade in the eighteenth century served parts of this process, especially the growing of sugar cane on Caribbean islands and of cotton in North America.

Much of the imperial venture was pursued by private companies that sent ships to distant parts of the world for trade. In England these included: the East India Company (or EIC, founded in 1600), which traded with points east of the Cape of Good Hope, including India, present-day Indonesia and China; the Hudson's Bay Company (founded in 1670), which traded with North America; and the Royal African Company, founded in 1672 with a statutory charter granting it 'the whole, entire and only trade for buying and selling bartering and exchanging of for or with any Negroes, slaves, goods, wares, merchandise whatsoever' on the western side of Africa, in a sort of public–private partnership explicitly supporting English colonial plantations in America.[1] Among the commodities it acquired, the most important were gold, ivory and copper. Each of these companies required a charter from the monarch but conducted its affairs autonomously; the British state did not take control of India from the EIC until after the so-called Indian Mutiny of 1857, a full century after British forces had achieved military dominance there. Britain's trade with India, its most prized imperial possession, there-fore developed for two and a half centuries before the sub-continent became British colonial territory. These trading relations gradually evolved into imperial control, but they were backed up by military force from the beginning. And not only by the British, as explained here:

> No real attempt was made by the Europeans to trade on local terms and it was a given that trade-related violence was acceptable. K. N. Chaud[h]uri, author of *Trade and Civilization in the Indian Ocean*, argues: 'the principle of armed trading introduced by the Portu-guese conquistadors in the Indian Ocean was taken over by the Dutch and English East India companies without any attempt to find an explicit justification for the practice'.[2]

The most notorious of such exchanges was the 'triangular trade', which transported cotton and sugar eastwards across the Atlantic to the UK, took cotton textiles and other manufactured goods from Britain to West Africa for sale, and there acquired new slaves to work on the cotton and sugar plantations of North America and the Caribbean islands. Even without slavery, the inter-continental trade could end up impoverishing the non-European counterparts. The EIC's headquarters were set up in Kolkata, on the far side of India from Europe, because of the great riches to be found in that city's Bengali hinterland. According to one account:

> European warrior-merchants saw Bengal as one of the richest prizes in the world. An early English visitor described it as 'a wonderful land, whose richness and abundance neither war,

pestilence, nor oppression could destroy.' Well before, the Moroccan traveller Ibn Battuta had described Bengal as 'a country of great extent, and one in which rice is extremely abundant. Indeed, I have seen no region of the earth in which provisions are so plentiful.' In 1757, ... [Robert] Clive described the textile center of Dacca as 'extensive, populous, and rich as the city of London'... Bengal was known for its fine cotton ... and for the excellence of its textiles.[3]

However, by 1840 Dhaka's population had fallen from 150,000 to 30,000, as Charles Trevelyan, a senior EIC official, testified: 'The jungle and malaria are fast encroaching.... Dacca, the Manchester of India, has fallen from a very flourishing town to a very poor and small town.'[4] Why was this, when the original purpose of the British presence was to acquire luxuries produced in Bengal? After Clive had secured military control of the region for Britain in the previous century,

> British traders, using 'every conceivable form of roguery,' 'acquired the weavers' cloth for a fraction of its value,' English merchant William Bolts wrote in 1772. 'Various and innumerable are the methods of oppressing the poor weavers ... such as by fines, imprisonments, floggings, forcing bonds from them, etc.' 'The oppression and monopolies' imposed by the English 'have been the causes of the decline of trade, the decrease of the revenues, and the present ruinous condition of affairs in Bengal.'[5]

So after military control was secured, Bengal was impoverished by being forced to export its wares to Britain at knockdown prices. This was then capped with the industrialization of Britain's own cloth production, which, allied to the cheap cultivation of cotton by slave labour, transformed the economics of textiles, in which India (and Bengal in particular) had previously excelled: 'The marriage of the new steam and spinning technologies was consummated by the installation of a steam engine in a spinning factory in Nottinghamshire in 1785. This led to a radical reduction in the cost of spun yarn which by 1812 was only one-tenth of its cost three decades before.'[6] The Indian market was opened up for cheap imports from Britain:

The free influx of English textiles began in 1813.... It is estimated that the de-industrialization effect of the forced free trade was equivalent to 55 to 75 per cent of the national consumption of India by 1870–80, reaching 95 to 99 per cent in 1890–1900 – or near-total destruction of the local industry ... other industries which became exposed to imports from Britain suffered the same fate.[7]

Africa scrambled

In Africa, colonization had more complex origins. Since it happened at a time when European colonialism was already mature, it is considered less likely that economic factors played a large part in the late-nineteenth-century 'Scramble for Africa':

> It is true that the African colonies supplied raw materials (metals, food stuffs, timber etc.), but they never became the markets for manufactured goods that some had hoped for. The colonies were expensive to administer and expensive to defend. They never really made any money. As a famous English historian, A. J. P. Taylor, wrote after the Second World War: 'Tot up the national balance sheet of any imperial country over the last fifty years and you will find the community is staggeringly out of profit.'[8]

Yet during 75 years of European rule the economy of Africa was remodelled like no other. Unlike British rule in India, the continent was divided into dozens of colonies and protectorates, each of them separately administered even when two neighbours were controlled by the same European state. They may not have offered rich markets but they did supply many commodities to Europe, such as copper from the Congo and Zambia, gold and cocoa from Ghana, and palm oil from Nigeria. A modern commercial economy was forced upon Africa even more brutally and rapidly than it had been on Bengal, making each colony or protectorate face outwards towards European and global markets. Such transport, trade and other communications as were developed linked each territory, or parts of it, to the African coast and the outside world rather than to neighbouring colonies or even other regions of the same territory.

Africa's tragedy is that after the end of slavery in the early nineteenth century, and during the later period of European empires, it found itself in the worst of all worlds: territorially fragmented, it was ruled by foreign powers directly to facilitate the extraction of wealth wherever possible; and it did not meanwhile develop the local markets that existed elsewhere. This is what Africa's new rulers took on with independence between the 1950s and the 1970s; and we will see recent parallels with that process as this book progresses.

It has been pointed out that 'Some of the biggest overseas profits were made in countries which were not colonised. China, Persia, the Ottoman Empire, Brazil and Argentina, for example, offered some of the best sources of raw materials and markets for manufactured goods, without Europeans having to pay the costs of colonisation.'[9] In some of these places, the European presence had consequences just as devastating for local trade as in Bengal. An example is the damage wrought in the nineteenth century by Britain's Opium Wars in China – described by Adam Smith in the previous century as 'a country much richer than any part of Europe'.[10] As in India before 1857, actual colonization was not necessary for an unbalanced relationship of power and commerce to develop.

In the 1970s a comparable modern phenomenon was explained by a set of explanations which is loosely described as 'dependency theory';[11] it was swept aside in the ideological fervour for the free market a decade later, but without ever being seriously refuted. The interplay of private trade and military enforcement, without actual colonization, continues in places as before – as this description of the modern oil industry in Nigeria shows, drawing the historical parallel explicitly:

> For twelve years, [Nigel Watson-Clark] saw active military service as a British Royal Marine.... After leaving the Marines he took, ... in 2002, a job in Nigeria ... his main concern was protecting Shell's ... floating oil platform ... some seven miles offshore....
>
> Shell controls over 50 percent of the oil and gas reserves in the country. Shell's corporate fate and that of Nigeria are thus intertwined....

Colonizing powers have always used armed forces to protect their commercial assets in the [Niger] Delta. . . . Soldiers were employed by the Royal Navy and sent to protect ships of the Royal African Company, which were transporting slaves from the creeks of the Delta to the American colonies. . . . After slavery came palm oil plantations. Now the exploited resources are oil and gas.[12]

A foot on the accelerator

The unequal relationships of power and commerce were greatly reinforced by the global policies imposed on all the weaker developing countries from the 1980s. The dominant philosophy of development had altered abruptly after a change of thinking at the World Bank in the early 1980s. Policy paths pursued in the 1960s and 1970s, and favoured by the majority of the world's nations, were replaced by policies made at the International Monetary Fund (IMF) and the World Bank, in which developed countries (mainly the United States) hold the great majority of votes. The two organizations' headquarters stand opposite each other, a short walk away from the White House in Washington; and while, according to a so far unbroken convention, the managing director of the IMF is always a European, the World Bank's president is always a US citizen, nominated by the US President himself.

And so what came to be known as the Washington Consensus was born. Its market-led, export-oriented philosophy has been entrenched steadily ever since, acquiring during the course of the 1990s the name of 'globalization'. The theoretical origin of the change in thinking lay in a report on Africa written for the World Bank in 1981 by a team led by a US economist, Elliot Berg. Drawing on the abstractions of economic theory and lacking any historical perspective, the report said that 'accelerated development' could be achieved if both international and domestic markets affecting African countries were freed up, enabling price mechanisms to operate better. It was necessary to remove market 'distortions' that arose from protective tariffs and other 'obstacles' to trade, such as government-run export marketing boards.[13] This, it was argued, would ensure that resources were allocated in the most efficient manner, and as a result African countries would be able to compete better on world markets. An essential element lay in redressing the balance between the urban and rural economies, which, it was claimed, were distorted in favour of the cities and industry.

It was not just later, in the light of events, that this approach came to be criticized: it was subject to a prolonged critique during the 1980s. A contemporary reviewer of the report wrote that Elliot Berg had 'inflicted his ideological preference for market economics on more aid programs to Africa than probably any other Westerner in the last decade'. The reviewer argued that, when African finance ministers had asked for a discussion of what the World Bank could do in the 1980s to enhance African development, 'What they received, instead, is a study of what African governments should do to promote Western capital.' The report advised that African public sectors were overextended as governments wasted resources on organizing, motivating and controlling people, a job which the market would do far more efficiently. It insisted that an export-led model for agricultural growth was the only viable one and thus, the reviewer reported, the Bank 'seeks reforms in macroeconomic policies – such as disbanding state marketing boards and devaluing the currency – to conform to the model'.[14]

Africa's governments were so incensed by the Berg Report that they signed a statement at the World Bank's annual meeting in 1981 which 'deplored the tendency in the study to link aid to the acceptance of a certain type of development model'.[15] The previous year they had produced their own Lagos Plan of Action, which set out a quite different path of development for their continent over the ensuing 20 years.[16] The most important item in implementing the Plan was to be the creation by 2000 of an African Economic Community 'so as to ensure the economic, social and cultural integration of our continent'.[17] Yet it is only *since* 2000 – when the long, sorry episode of the Washington Consensus and structural adjustment was already peetering out – that regional integration in Africa has finally appeared on the agenda of international institutions. It is an apt reflection of the two documents that, more than a quarter of a century later, it is easier to find a copy of the Lagos Plan on the Internet than it is to call up the far more influential Berg Report.

The report led to a change not just in the World Bank's thinking about development but also in its role. The Bank moved into the policy field. Rather than lending for specific objects such as ports and dams, much as a commercial bank might do, the Bank decided that policy guidance in favour of the new pro-market approach was required. Economic structures that got in the way of the market had to be reformed or removed, and the Bank created structural adjustment loans in order to advise countries how to change their economic systems in order to respond better to international price signals. The first such loan was granted to Turkey in March 1980, and soon they became commonplace throughout the Bank's areas of operation, including countries at much lower levels of development than Turkey. This began the process of linking aid to a certain type of development model, as the African governments complained in 1981. Critics have long since derided this practice as 'one size fits all', a comment on the refusal to tailor structural adjustment and the International Monetary Fund's economic stabilization programmes to the needs, possibilities and political preferences of the countries to which they are applied.

The Berg Report was closely followed by the onset of the international debt crisis in 1982, which greatly helped efforts to change the conceptual climate. The response to the debt crisis gave the IMF influence over a great many more countries than before. The IMF required countries to undergo economic stabilization programmes as a condition of receiving its loans. These were used to support the call to replace the import substitution policies of the biggest debtors, such as Brazil and Argentina, and to open their economies up to international competition and world market prices. The programmes required the sharp reduction of tariffs and removal of other 'barriers' to free interplay with world markets as well as the reduction of public spending, especially in 'unproductive' areas such as health and education.[18] But it was the Bank that mainly proselytized this way of thinking, summing up the aim in a slogan, 'Get the prices right'.

Debtor countries were required to accept the IMF's pro-grammes before the creditors would revise their loan repayment schedules. This forced on the developing countries a huge loss of sovereignty and self-respect barely a generation after most of them had won their independence. Developing countries as a whole have only recently begun to recover their morale, regaining some confidence since 2001 while defending their policy positions during the protracted Doha Round negotiations of the World Trade Organization (WTO).

The IMF had never been conceived of as a development institution. Despite the rhetoric on both sides of the argument, its loan programmes and policy conditions contained only the broadest hints of a development strategy that could supplant Africa's Lagos Plan and the national plans that many countries had previously adopted. This oversight could be (and still is) defended with the doctrinaire argument that markets would automatically stimulate economic growth once they were freed from restraints. There is, however, little historical evidence for such an assertion. Markets do not exist in a legal, social and political vacuum; they are built everywhere on a framework of policies, laws and social conventions.

The export orientation trap

However, the World Bank's principles of the 1980s did provide the outline of a strategy: its most important element was that countries should cease trying to produce substitutes for imports and instead concentrate on exports in order to earn foreign currency and balance their trade. As we have seen, most developing countries export either agricultural or mineral commodities. It was argued that, unlike import substitution, the strategy of export orientation would provide domestic businesses with the disciplines of the market to enable them to become internationally competitive. An attendant requirement was for governments to reduce their import tariffs, which would expose suppliers on their domestic markets to foreign competition at the ruling international prices, and so encourage them to match it for productivity and costs.

The Bank published what amounted to a policy manifesto for agriculture and trade in its annual *World Development Report* in 1986. The report attacked at length what it called the taxation of agricultural exports, both actual and implicit: 'Some taxation of export crops involves conventional border taxes or quotas, but frequently taxation is a result of the pricing policies pursued by marketing agencies in the public sector.'[19] State commodity marketing boards were therefore among the first targets of the reduction in government's role.

Right from the beginning many commentators argued that the doctrine of export orientation was fallible. The thinking behind it depended on the economic theory of comparative advantage, according to which all countries will be better off if each one specializes in whatever it produces most efficiently. However, the Bank's interpretation of the theory was static: that countries should concentrate on their existing strengths rather than try to develop new ones in more diverse and advanced areas of activity. Countries with a comparative advantage in export crops were expected to exploit it, and use the commercial proceeds to import food if need be. But development is a dynamic process, requiring of necessity that new branches of the economy be set up. Even if the theory of comparative advantage is accepted (and it is by no means universally accepted as a guide for development), for policy purposes it has to be interpreted in a dynamic way, encouraging a country to develop more advanced sectors which will help it to climb up the ladder of development. This requires a national readiness to take risks with new ventures – a habit of mind that the bureaucrats at the Bank seemed to prefer to stifle, for all their supposed attachment to entrepreneurship and markets, even though it probably entails an even greater economic risk to pursue the static approach to comparative advantage, and keep the country that follows it stuck in its existing groove.

Economists also warned of a 'fallacy of composition' (or 'adding-up problem') in the doctrine of export-led growth. One country facing balance of payments difficulties might do well out of advice to export more of its main traded product. However, if the

Table 3 Average world primary commodity prices over three-year periods, 1977—9 and 2004—6

Commodity group	Unit of price (in current US dollars unless indicated)	1977—9	2004—6	Changes in average real prices* from 1977—9 to 2004—6, %
All commodities	Index[†]	116	124	− 31
All commodities (in SDRs)	Index	124	113	− 42
Food and tropical beverages	Index	129	116	− 45
Tropical beverages	Index	252	107	−74
Coffee	c/lb	184.62	82.42	−77
Cocoa	c/lb	158.50	70.75	−76
Tea	Index	86	82	−44
Food	Index	115	117	−38
Sugar	c/lb	8.53	10.61	−33
Beef	c/lb	98.8	116.3	−37
Maize	$/metric ton	104	111	−43
Wheat	$/metric ton	133	173	−32
Rice	$/metric ton	325	279	−54
Bananas	c/lb	13.37	26.99	+ 9
Vegetable oilseeds and oils	Index	169	144	−53
Soya beans	$/metric ton	282	283	−46
Agricultural raw materials	Index	103	123	−28
Cotton	c/lb	73.41	58.01	−58
Tobacco	US import unit value	2,289	2,833	−33
Rubber	$/metric ton	1,031.2	1,638.0	−14
Tropical logs	$/cu.m.	197.3	328.7	−10
Minerals, ores and metals	Index	86	136	+ 23
Aluminium	$/metric ton	1,193.0	2,061.2	−7
Phosphate rock	$/metric ton	35.33	42.39	−35
Iron ore	c/Fe unit	22.74	57.78	+ 37
Tin	$/metric ton	13,025	8,221	−66
Copper	$/metric ton	1,552.1	4,422.0	+ 54
Tungsten ore	$/10 kg WO3	151.10	114.35	−59
Gold	$/troy ounce	215.88	486.10	+ 21
Crude petroleum	$/barrel	18.34	51.81	+ 52

Sources: Adapted from Table 1.A1 in UNCTAD (2006b), with further data added from *Beyond 20/20 WDS*, «stats.unctad.org/Handbook/TableViewer/tableView.aspx», Table 6.1 and the World Bank's Commodity Price Data sheets, and calculations by the author. Maize price data are from IMF and International Rice Research Institute.

* Actual prices deflated by the export unit value of manufactured goods from developed countries, which stood at 64.4 in 1977–9 and at 119.4 in 2004–6, against the base year of 2000 = 100.

† For all indices, the base year is 2000 (= 100).

same advice was heeded simultaneously by several countries, the market would be flooded with supplies and the price would collapse. The severity and rapidity of that collapse would vary only with the extent to which demand for the product responded to price changes – its elasticity of demand, in economists' language. If demand is inelastic, or other negative factors intervene along the supply chain, producers' total earnings on the market will fall even while export volumes increase.

This is precisely what happened in several markets that are of importance to numerous developing countries. On some markets the total value of international trade declined, alongside a large increase in traded volumes. For example, world coffee exports increased from 3.7 million metric tons in 1980 to 5.9 million tons in 2000, but their total value declined from US$12.5 billion to $10.2 billion in the same years. Over the same period cocoa exports more than doubled from 1.1 million to 2.5 million tons but, with production persistently exceeding demand, their value fell from $2.8 billion to $2.5 billion;[20] between 1977 and 2001 the real price of cocoa fell at the rate of 6.9 per cent per year.[21]

Over a long period there was a substantial fall in nearly all international commodity prices, although much of it was disguised by the violent ups and downs that also characterize those markets. In Table 3 we see that, on average, the US dollar prices of internationally traded commodities fell by 31 per cent between the years 1977–9 and 2004–6, when set against the prices of the manufactured goods that developing countries import. Moreover, these average real commodity prices fell over this period by as much as 42 per cent when expressed in Special Drawing Rights (SDRs, a fictitious composite currency designed by the IMF). And this percentage is more representative of international reality than dollar prices, since the SDR combines the values of all the leading currencies in the developed world; and the dollar has fallen in value against the others since the 1970s. This will be examined in detail in Chapter 3. In many cases the prices received by farmers have fallen even further than this, while the prices of the same goods (or those processed from them) have held up much better at the point of retail sale in the importing countries. This will be further discussed in Chapter 4.

The fallacy of composition was horribly illustrated by recent events in the vanilla trade. In 2005, farmers in Uganda were reported to have resumed planting upland rice instead of vanilla, after the vanilla price collapsed in a classic market crash. According to one report, local prices received by farmers fell from Ush150,000 per kg of vanilla in 2003 to just Ush500 in 2005 – if there were any buyers at all. Vanilla processers were hesitant to buy because they had not yet sold off the previous year's crop and most had not received any new buying orders at all.

The background lay in a series of crises in Madagascar, which usually produces up to half of the world's natural vanilla output. In 1994, the IMF required Madagascar to abandon price controls on vanilla while the nation's vanilla reserves, amounting to 2,000 tons, were sold. But Madagascar is very vulnerable to cyclones and, in 2000, one quarter of the national crop was destroyed in a cyclone, along with more than 100 tons waiting for export. With no reserves to replace this loss of supplies, the international price went up from US$20 per kg in 1999 to $33 in 2000, and then soared to a reported peak of about $450 per kg in 2004, after a political crisis in Madagascar in 2002 further disrupted production; prices for the best vanilla pods were reported as high as $500–$600 per kg.

In 2004, the IMF urged Madagascar to take advantage of the high price and grow more vanilla. It does not seem to have been aware that the price surge was already having two entirely predictable consequences. On the demand side, vanilla users substituted cheaper artificial vanillin flavour, while on the supply side new growers entered the market in such countries as India and Papua-New Guinea in addition to Uganda. Many of them had removed coffee trees to plant supposedly more remunerative vanilla instead. With several countries harvesting vanilla for the first time, world natural vanilla demand in 2004–5 was estimated at around 1,200 tons, but production was at 2,300 tons. The largest consuming firm, McCormick in the US, had stocked up as the price rose in 2003.[22] The international price plummeted and by 2006 gourmet-grade vanilla was selling at $20–$25 per kg. Prices paid to farmers for unprocessed green vanilla beans fell to $1–$1.50 per kg.[23]

Running on the spot

Put at its simplest, export orientation has forced the poorest countries to run ever faster in order to stay where they are. We see in Table 4 that between 1981–2 and 2001–3, LDCs' average export prices fell by 35.2 per cent in relation to their import prices. This means that by the end of that period their exports could pay for less than two-thirds as much in imports as at the beginning; in order again to import the same quantity of goods, they had to export *more than half as much again*. This relationship between export and import prices is called a country's terms of trade. The terms of trade for countries in sub-Saharan Africa (SSA), on average, deteriorated over this period by more than 20 per cent. Developing countries in general experienced a deterioration in their terms of trade but the developed countries benefited from an 8 per cent improvement.

It is no exaggeration therefore to say that, as a result of policies imposed to concentrate on production for export, these countries have experienced a grave *weakening* of their trading position. The process was different, but the outcome bears disturbing resemblances to the trade pattern imposed on India by the East

Table 4 Changes in terms of trade of some country groups, 1980–2 to 2001–3

Economy	Annual average, 1980–2	Annual average, 2001–3	% change from 1980–2 to 2001–3
Developed economies	95.7	103.3	+ 7.9
Developing economies	117.3	97.7	−16.7
Developing economies: Africa	131.7	100.0	−24.1
Least developed countries	144.0	93.3	−35.2
Landlocked countries	114.7	96.3	−16.0
Sub-Saharan Africa	124.0	98.3	−20.7

Source: Calculated from UNCTAD, «stats.unctad.org/Handbook/TableViewer/tableView.aspx», Table 2.1. Base year: 2000 = 100

India Company in the late eighteenth century. For the poorest countries, export orientation has resulted in a vicious circle of debts, food deficits and declining incomes. But the recent history of China gives us another reminder of the usual relationship of successful development policies with agriculture and poverty, as we read: '[T]he bulk of poverty reduction in China occurred during the phase of agricultural de-collectivization and increases in food prices procurement before 1980, rather than in the subsequent trade opening phase.'[24]

Let us think for a moment about the policy dilemma poor countries now face. Take an indebted country that relies on agricultural commodities for its exports and finds that the long-term revenue from them is falling. How can it keep its imports up (including much of the food consumed by its people) and also pay off its external debts? Perhaps it should increase those exports further, in order to earn more foreign exchange. This is the export orientation line. But if the prices have been falling, it is actually more difficult for its farmers to buy the extra inputs required to increase their output on existing land; in some countries farmers have not been applying any chemicals to their land or trees in any case, and so they can scarcely increase their production per hectare. The only alternative will be to devote more land to export crops. But that land (unless taken from uncultivated forest or savannah, with attendant environmental risks) could otherwise grow food for domestic consumption. And if land previously used for domestic food production is given over to exports, then either food imports must also increase or there will be growing food shortages and malnutrition. And so the vicious circle is closed.

Small-scale farmers are faced with a similar dilemma to the national one. Some have responded by replacing conventional crops such as coffee with the more remunerative cultivation of narcotics like coca (if they live in Colombia), chat (also known as *khat*, in Ethiopia) and heroin poppies (in Afghanistan).

But no country can live without trade, and a North Korean-style closed economy is not the answer either. Every country has to earn foreign currency, if only to pay for necessary imports. It will always need to import some goods and services from elsewhere; and the smaller it is and the less diverse its economy, the greater the variety of imports it is likely to require. At the simplest, every country needs to import some raw materials and other supplies to keep its existing economy going. This might mean metals and oil products for industry and transport, and other inputs for agriculture. If the country is also to develop its infrastructure and public services, for example by building roads, schools and clinics, or installing water supplies, it will need appropriate supplies and quite possibly specialized foreign personnel too. Likewise, the development of industry and of currency earners such as tourism will require the import of machinery and other supplies and equipment. Some consumer goods will also be imported, as well as food. All of this has to be paid for in foreign currency, which must be earned from exports and other receipts from abroad.

It has become urgent to find a way out of this impasse, which explains much of the downward economic spiral reported in Chapter 1. The priority given by foreign aid donors to exports, rather than food security, has led many poor countries directly into this trap. Yet bizarrely, the years of structural adjustment also witnessed a sharp *fall* in foreign aid for agriculture and rural development, in spite of complaints about a presumed urban bias in the previous era.

Global trade policies must also share responsibility for the disaster. The new doctrines were reinforced by an international treaty when the General Agreement on Tariffs and Trade (GATT) was supplemented by several additional agreements under the WTO, which started in 1995. Besides expanding the membership of the GATT (which regulates import tariffs and quantitative restrictions on trade), the WTO introduced rules in many new areas which severely limited the freedom of manoeuvre in development policy. Examples are the TRIMS agreement on investment measures, which outlawed development-related requirements on foreign investment of the sort even Margaret Thatcher's government had imposed on Japanese car companies in the UK in the 1980s; and the TRIPS agreement, which has been described as a form of corporate protectionism because it extends throughout the WTO's membership requirements on things like patents, copyrights and trademarks which used to be subject only to national rules.

Moreover, the liberalization of trade on the import side has in many cases undercut domestic agricultural prices, making it even harder for a country to feed its people off its own land. First IMF stabilization programmes and then, since 1995, the WTO have required developing countries to reduce duties and quantitative limits on their imports, including necessities such as food. Besides the consequences for agriculture, this has had serious implications for government revenues: the simplicity and reliability of import duties make them a favoured form of taxation in poor countries. In the 1930s, the policies pursued by many richer countries to cope with the Great Depression were described as 'beggar-my-neighbour': each country would devalue its currency in order to improve its trade position, but that made it more difficult for its neighbours to export their goods and prompted them also to devalue, and so on in a downward spiral. The policies we have described have a similar effect as each country's exports spoil foreign markets for its neighbours, and all of them end up worse off – the country pursuing these policies is beggared as inevitably as its neighbours.

Squeezed out of markets

The combination of export orientation, loss of direct government involvement and lack of any domestic influence over international trade has left the poorest countries vulnerable to the most damaging consequences of their dependence on small numbers of commodity markets. Indeed, they have been progressively frozen out of many traditional export markets. This happened first with metals and minerals. The mining industry used to be a mainstay of several poor countries' economies, especially in Africa, but it largely abandoned them in spite of the presence of rich mineral deposits. Africa ceased to be a great metal-mining continent.

This explains many of the recent difficulties of countries that were traditionally dependent on metals and minerals exports. Oil and mining companies have a great deal more choice over where to invest than farmers have, and in recent times their judgements of costs and risks made them noticeably less willing to operate in the poorest countries. To cite one major market, Chile has come to dominate copper mining while other, poorer but equally long-established centres such as Zambia and the Congo were eclipsed. Chile increased its share of an expanding world copper market from 13 per cent in 1978 to 29 per cent in 1997, while Africa's mine production of the metal fell by 52 per cent over the same period. In 1960, Africa was the second continent for copper mine production after North America; by 1997, it was equal fifth with Oceania[25] and by 2003 its share of world copper exports had fallen to just 2 per cent.[26] Zambia therefore fell into a spiral of decline earlier than agricultural exporting countries, since it had mistakenly assumed on independence in 1964 that copper would continue to provide a reliable source of foreign exchange and a basis for development. There were several reasons for the Congo's economic collapse over the same period, but in that country too this was one of the most important.

There are signs that this trend is going into reverse, at any rate in Africa. Gold production revived in Ghana quite a few years ago, while there has been much reporting of Chinese investment in Angolan oil[27] and in other ventures, and of other prospects such as the discovery of oil in Uganda, probably in commercial quantities.[28] Elsewhere new mines are planned, such as a nickel–cobalt mine in Madagascar that could nearly triple the country's merchandise exports.[29] The macroeconomic benefits are to be welcomed, while the environmental and social problems that often arise from oil drilling and metal mining will have to be assessed on their merits. But none of this can repair the economic damage already caused by the sharp reduction in such activity in previous decades; in many countries it is unlikely to go into reverse.

The decline of the mining sector was an important creator of poverty in countries that used to depend on such industries. By the late 1990s, among six categories of LDC by export specialization, the mineral-exporting countries showed the highest incidences of poverty, with 82 per cent of their people living in 1997–9 on less than US$1 a day and 94 per cent on less than US$2 a day. In 1981–3 the respective figures in the same countries had been 61 per cent and 87 per cent.[30] Among the six categories, the mineral exporters were the only countries in which the real value of exports actually declined between the 1980s and the 1990s, at a rate of 1.9 per cent per year. Among those specializing in agricultural exports, by contrast, real exports expanded at 6.3 per cent per year.[31] The seven countries in the mineral-exporting category included three (DR Congo, Liberia and Sierra Leone) that have suffered major civil wars: was the collapse of the state the cause of their economic distress, as is often suggested, or a consequence of it?

In consequence, agriculture now assumes a much greater role in these countries than in the past. But where agricultural markets are oversupplied, poor countries are being squeezed out of them too, as purchasers have more supplier options. They tend to prefer suppliers in countries that are not only larger (and capable of supplying greater quantities) and more accessible, but offer better facilities and better product quality, physical infrastructure and support for commerce. In these circumstances, less poor countries tend to be preferred to the very poorest; and corporate market concentration at one end of the supply chain and national concentration at the other become mutually reinforcing. For example, on the coffee market the three biggest suppliers (Brazil, Vietnam and Colombia) are of greater interest to roaster companies than smaller, more remote countries in Africa and elsewhere. By 2005 Africa's share of world coffee exports had fallen to barely half what it had been only ten years earlier, while that of the LDCs fell by more than one-third.[32] This seriously compounded the effects for both African countries and LDCs of a 77 per cent decline in real coffee prices since the late 1970s. We will examine these questions further in Chapter 4.

There are further constraints on poor farmers' ability to obtain the best prices for their produce and to exploit opportunities that arise. These are the consequences of many things: inadequate infrastructure, especially in roads and transport; small and remote farms facing a greater number of intermediaries on the way to the export port than do larger farms in more prosperous countries; insufficient support for farmers in the form of extension services and other sources of knowledge; and lack of access at affordable prices to inputs such as seeds and fertilizers. All of this prevents the poorest countries from making the best use of the commodity markets. For all these reasons, when world coffee prices were at their lowest between 2000 and 2002, producers in LDCs of the less-sought-after robusta variety were paid on average 17 US cents per pound of coffee beans, compared with 25 cents to producers in other developing countries; while LDC producers of the higher-grade arabica variety received 37 cents per pound, compared with 69 cents elsewhere.[33] Meanwhile, many attempts to diversify have been frustrated, either because the price of the new crop itself declined or because access to the market was denied due to import barriers, subsidies to domestic producers or other commercial or regulatory restrictions. We saw what happened in the case of vanilla.

The structure of many of the poorest countries' economies has also degenerated. For example, the trend in many of them has been *away from* diversification, not towards it: among LDCs, processed primary commodities fell from 24.5 per cent of commodity-sector exports in 1981–3 to 11.1 per cent in 1997–9. Processed minerals, metals and fuels fell from 20.8 per cent to 12.1 per cent of commodity-sector exports among non-oil commodity-exporting LDCs.[34]

This is partly the consequence of trade liberalization, which exposed local processing industries to competition from imports: as in Bengal in the nineteenth century, many of them were not able to withstand it. But there have been other causes. In one reported attack on export taxes, the World Bank in 1995 required Mozambique to reduce a tax on raw cashew nut exports. This had the anticipated effect of raising raw cashew prices, including the farmers' share of the price. However, it also led to the closure of cashew-nut processing factories and the loss of about 10,000 Mozambican jobs, since it ignored the incentive that the tax gave to export the nuts in processed form. According to one account, 'The cashew sector went from being a net exporter of processed cashew to a net exporter of raw cashew' – leaving a reduction in value added and a small step *down* the ladder of development. Moreover, an export cartel developed, controlling the prices paid to farmers, while the raw cashew exports in turn went to a tightly controlled market in India. Those who enjoyed market power (the export cartel and the monopolistic importer) were therefore reported to be the main beneficiaries of the policy change.[35]

Blaming the poor's rulers

Since the turn of the millennium the policy principles enunciated in the 1980s have been modified. The Washington Consensus was succeeded by what came to be known, rather awkwardly, as a 'Post-Washington Consensus'. In this, as in Berg's time, the failings of poor countries are largely attributed to their own governments. This is despite the loss of national control over policy which came with structural adjustment and IMF loan conditionality. But the criticisms made of the governments go further than they did then: the fault is no longer said to lie in the wrong policies but in the whole system of 'governance' (to use the vogue word). It is however not clear what the desired system of governance is. In public discourse the emphasis is generally laid on avoiding corruption and observing human rights and democracy; but while certainly desirable in themselves, the nature of the link between those virtues and economic development seems somewhat obscure, considering that China's economic progress has been accompanied by a poor record on precisely those scores; and history shows China to be far from unique in that respect. However, in the policies actually pursued under aid programmes, the emphasis of governance tends to be placed once again on reducing the size of the state and promoting a free-market economy.

According to one critical African observer, the concept of 'good governance' was promoted by the IMF and World Bank precisely in order to explain the failure of structural adjustment programmes (SAPs). Very conveniently, it also provides an excuse to extend rich nations' political control over poor countries even further. As this observer wrote, the idea was

> that SAPs have failed, in large part, because African States are 'corrupt', 'wasteful' and 'rent-seeking' and because of the 'poor implementation' of policies. In other words, SAPs were basically 'sound', it is the combination of 'rampant corruption' and lack of qualified personnel that led to the failure of these policies.[36]

Many a rich-world politician or newspaper columnist now feeds the impression that a crisis of poverty affects Africa alone, and that it arises from internal politics in that continent, benighted as it is said to be by corruption, incompetence and inefficiency. These failings certainly exist in Africa – just as they do in many other parts of the world, including some countries which are very rich. Many of the leading developed countries were themselves corrupt or authoritarian during their periods of economic transformation. In the late eighteenth and early nineteenth centuries the United Kingdom's ruling class was actually nicknamed Old Corruption, and the United States a hundred years later was scarcely better. In that period the UK was not only corrupt but more repressive than in any recent period of its history, as its government struggled to contain any sympathies with the French Revolution. Other countries have been authoritarian at similar stages in their development: for example, the military government of South Korea in the 1970s and 1980s, before industrial strikes precipitated that country's democratization; and China throughout the last 30 years, although there are signs that it too may be beginning to ease up under the pressures of industrialization and urbanization. By contrast, in the final years of the USSR, political liberalization *preceded* the botched liberal market reforms of the 1990s; as a consequence of the latter, democracy was discredited in people's minds and it has weakened in recent years, just as economic performance has picked up.

Rather as in Victorian England, these arguments seem to depict poverty as the fault of poor people – or at least, that of the rulers of poor countries. Witness this account of World Bank-associated corruption:

> From big multimillion-dollar contracts to daily transactions through general cash accounts, project officials [of developing countries] have concocted all sorts of scams to embezzle Bank funds. With or without the aid of accomplices on the outside, they establish shell companies, facilitate bid rigging, create fraudulent procurement documents, establish hidden project accounts, authorize payments for overpriced goods and services, and commit other fraudulent acts to enrich themselves. [37]

The author, a former World Bank official, estimated that the Bank 'has lost $100 billion from its portfolio through fraud and corruption, and it may possibly have lost even more'. [38] But his account does not try to explain the economic background to such behaviour, which derives from the huge gulf in resources between the World Bank (and other aid donors) and the countries where they operate. To give an example from my own experience as project manager of a British government agricultural reform project in Russia in the late 1990s: my Russian deputy's pay was less than one-eighth of mine, although his job was every bit as demanding and responsible. He was scrupulously honest, but if he had not been one would have understood the sources of temptation. If private enterprise is about finding opportunities for profitable activity, where better to exercise such talents in a poor country than in a rich foreign organization which, moreover, exists on the pretext of giving?

Plan for development

Nevertheless, there is ample evidence that, for development to succeed, a certain political attitude *is* required of a country's leaders. But it is not the willingness to open all doors to foreign capital and trade that is advocated as 'good governance'. On the contrary, the required political stance tends to give primacy to domestic economic forces and to protect them for an extended period from foreign competition, so that they can accumulate the capital and experience needed for further advance. It also recognizes the importance of agricultural production and food security, partly for the people's own well-being but also to insulate the country from the pressures that can arise from food shortages and imports. I shall have more to say about this in Chapter 5.

Before the 1980s all of this was well understood in development circles. The recent success of both India and China can be ascribed largely to their adherence to these principles, including their determination to produce their own food after the harsh experience of famine in previous decades. Broadly speaking, these were also the policies of the British government before it went over to free agricultural trade in 1846, while Germany adopted a similar approach explicitly as it industrialized during the nineteenth century. In the United States, industrialization was achieved under the shelter of what were, until the 1930s, the highest industrial tariffs in the world;[39] the only break in them came 'when the country tried to liberalize prematurely in 1847–61, the industrial sector suffered and the country had to revert to protectionism against imports from Great Britain'[40] (besides which, it fell into a civil war). Japanese policy after the Second World War was comparable, as were South Korea's for 20 years from the late 1960s, China's since Deng Hsiao-ping's first reforms in the late 1970s, and Malaysia consistently since independence in 1957. Much the same seems also to be true of President Putin's economic nationalism in Russia, by contrast with the disastrous free-for-all sponsored there by the IMF in the 1990s.

These notions were long ago given the name of the 'developmental state', an essential aspect of which lies in the readiness to *plan* economic developments. When asked recently for the reasons for Malaysia's relative success since independence, the country's trade and industry minister simply replied, 'Planning, planning, planning'.[41] Wider development policy there is guided by an Economic Planning Unit in the Prime Minister's Office and operates through regular development plans and a Long-term Industrial Master Plan. In the area of export commodities, there is a specific government ministry called the Ministry of Plantation Industries and Commodities, which used to be the Ministry of

Primary Industries and had the same minister from 1986 to 2004. Its goals include securing more attractive prices and focusing on value-added activities. As a former economics minister of Taiwan put it in 1981:

> Although the value of economic planning is still not accepted by some 'free market' economists, the impressive results that some countries have achieved through such planning cannot be denied.... [F]or developing countries, particularly those where the conditions required for the smooth operation of the market mechanism are absent or incomplete, the need for economic planning seems even greater than in the developed ones.[42]

Now, 'planning' is a controversial word in modern economic policy, but if we replace it with the phrase 'strategy, analysis and leadership', the point seems so obvious as to be hardly worth making. That, surely, is what governments are there to provide. The question is not whether they should do it, but how they should go about it and how well they achieve it. Each government must have sufficient policy space to pursue its own line of planning.

There are numerous states in Africa and other poor regions which could not be described as developmental. However, a contrary example is found in Botswana, which has enjoyed the fastest economic growth per head of any country in the world since it became independent in 1966. A combination of the social composition and traditions of Botswana's state and the commercial possibilities encountered after diamonds were discovered has more than compensated for the country's disadvantages of small size and a landlocked location. Careful state planning of the economy has been just as important to it as in Malaysia:

> Each [National Development Plan] would go forward to Parliament for debate and approval only after it had been debated within government and a consensus had been achieved. The final step in that process was a multi-day discussion in the Economic Committee of Cabinet, which ... was chaired by the president. Projects that could not be accommodated within the consensus plan could not be funded.[43]

As a group of African economists recently noted, Botswana also 'held successful initial negotiations with its diamond company, resulting in high levels of royalties, and *benefited from the controlled and stable nature of the world diamond market*'.[44] Mauritius's success as a developmental state also benefited from large guaranteed export quotas for its leading crop (sugar cane) to the EU over the last 30 years at up to three times world market prices, and for more than 20 years before that to the UK. The significance of internationally managed exports such as these will become apparent in the next chapter.

'Get the prices right' revisited

A quarter of a century after the big changes in World Bank policy, it is clear that there was no acceleration of development. The stated objective of structural adjustment was to increase efficiency by enabling markets to operate freely, but it was often followed by economic stagnation and even decline. As evidence, 10 of the 31 countries classed as of low human development are poorer now than they were before the Berg Report of 1981, and only 8 were at their richest in 2004, the latest year shown.[45]

In its policies since the 1980s the World Bank has aspired to a world in which there would be no barriers to trade, all markets would be connected and they would work efficiently to ensure a regular balance between supply and demand (what economists call 'market clearing'). In this ideal world, price signals were expected to lead to the most efficient allocation of resources, advancing the welfare of all concerned. This doctrine ignored the possibility that markets can fail to satisfy these requirements, as happened for example when the private sector did not provide for important ancillary functions of the former agricultural marketing boards, such as the provision of market information, research and agricultural extension. The Bank's policies affecting export commodities failed more comprehensively than most, partly because commodity markets themselves are well known to perform their functions as markets very poorly (as we shall see in Chapter 3).

Under the Post-Washington Consensus the level of policy ambition has been reduced as the emphasis now is on poverty reduction, not development; and there is no talk at all of 'accelerated' development. This has led to two important innovations. In 2000 the United Nations approved a set of 'Millennium Development Goals', which aimed to reduce the numbers of poor and hungry people to half of their 1990 levels by 2015. Meanwhile, a programme of foreign debt write-offs was introduced under the Highly Indebted Poor Countries (HIPC) initiative. Under the guise of handing control over policy back to national governments and people, this institutionalized a new form of policy conditionality in so-called Poverty Reduction Strategy Papers (PRSPs); no HIPC debt writedown can go ahead until the World Bank and the IMF have approved a PRSP for the country concerned. Despite the nominal focus on poverty, the PRSPs are far-reaching enough to provide the semblance of national development strategies. But the approach still in practice amounts to one-size-fits-all, the main difference being that the Bank- and Fund-approved policies are written up in words chosen by people of the applicant country. Just as in the governance agenda, the basics of structural adjustment are still in place: market liberalization, export orientation, a minimal economic role for the state, privatization and trade liberalization (which is code for reducing tariffs and other restrictions on imports).[46]

However, the HIPC debt write-offs, combined with richer (middle-income) developing countries' growing disdain for the IMF, have led the Fund into a serious financial crisis. There is also growing criticism of the World Bank Group for its habit of providing more aid to middle-income countries, which can afford to borrow at market rates of interest from its main body, the International Bank for Reconstruction and Development. The funds available to low-income countries at concessionary rates from its International Development Association arm are more limited.

This criticism is perhaps timely as, according to one summary, the evidence of economic deterioration in the era of structural adjustment overseen by the Washington twins 'includes declining

per capita income and food production, worsening balance of payments, growing domestic resource gaps, diminishing participation
in foreign direct investment flows and rising foreign debt'.[47] The
IMF in particular demonstrated a serious lack of grounding in the
realities of poor countries. Its policy of reducing border tariffs in
order to liberalize trade deprived their governments of an
important and easily collected form of revenue, and usually nothing
satisfactory was put in its place. The IMF has argued that tariffs
should either be replaced by value-added tax or other sales taxes
(which tend to affect poor people disproportionately and require
much more administration than import duties do), or be replaced
by no new fiscal source at all, in the hope that either foreign donors
or economic growth will make up the difference in the government's budget. This seems like the policy of pious hope. IMF data
themselves demonstrate that government revenues of low-income
countries have declined since the 1980s, almost entirely due to
reductions in tariffs; on the other hand, taxation in high-income
countries has continued to increase as a proportion of GDP over
this period (and they continued to prosper).[48]

In a long and detailed article published in 2004 (and already
quoted above), the Senegalese economist D. M. Dembele argued
that:

> Many African States have been stripped of all but a handful of their
> economic and social functions. . . . State retrenchment primarily
> aimed at eliminating subsidies for the poor, removing social
> protection, and abandoning its role in fighting for social justice
> through income redistribution and other social transfers to the
> most disadvantaged.[49]

Dembele's stark conclusion was that, 'The IMF and World Bank . . .
are instruments of domination and control in the hands of powerful
states whose long-standing objective is to perpetuate the plunder of
the resources of the Global South, especially Africa.' He echoed
Guy Gran (the 1982 reviewer of the Berg Report, who was quoted
earlier in this chapter) in his view that, 'The fundamental role of
the Bank and Fund in Africa and in the rest of the developing world
is to promote and protect the interests of global capitalism.'

Arguing that, 'They have never been interest[ed] in "reducing" poverty, much less in fostering "development"', Dembele concluded: 'If the experience of the last quarter of a century has taught Africa one fundamental lesson it is that the road to genuine recovery and development begins with a total break with the failed and discredited policies imposed by the IMF and the World Bank.'[50] It is an interesting fact that this article was quickly reproduced on websites all over Africa.

Markets, like economic processes of any sort, can only be means to development, not ends in themselves. They do not operate in a social or ethical void and in moral terms no price is either right or wrong in itself. A price's degree of rightness will depend on whose interests it best serves. The correct question to ask was not 'Are the prices right?' but 'Who are they right for, and why?' The right prices for development are those that enable the poorest countries, and the poorest citizens in them, to clamber out of poverty and begin to catch up with their more fortunate peers. Seen in that light, commodity prices for 20 years went very badly *wrong*, and with them the prospects of hundreds of millions of poor people who depend on them directly or indirectly for their livelihoods. Liberalizing such markets and leaving these people to fend for themselves was profoundly damaging and irresponsible – with grave insult added to this injury when it was done in the name of 'accelerated development'.

Notes

1   Quoted from «www.nationalarchives.gov.uk/pathways/blackhistory/africa_caribbean/britain_trade.htm».
2   Buckman (2005), p. 7.
3   Chomsky (1993), Chapter 1, Segment 4/12 («www.zmag.org/Chomsky/year/year-c01-s04.html»).
4   *Ibid*.
5   *Ibid*.
6   Buckman (2005), p. 12.
7   Shafaeddin (2006), p. 24, citing Bagchi (1982) and Bairoch (1992).
8   Open Door Web Site (2007).

9   *Ibid.* This refers to the time after Brazil and Argentina achieved their independence from Portugal and Spain respectively.

10 Smith (1982), Book I, Chapter XI, p. 345. Smith's An *Inquiry into the Nature and Causes of the Wealth of Nations* was first published in London in 1776.

11 Many of the leading thinkers of dependency theory were from Latin America, among them Fernando Henrique Cardoso (a sociologist who later became President of Brazil), Cristóbal Kay, Gabriel Palma and Osvaldo Sunkel. The origin of their ideas lay in the Latin American structuralist school of economics, of which the founding father was Raúl Prebisch. Some more radical (and widely publicized) members of the dependency school, such as André Gunder Frank, were closer to the Marxist tradition.

12 Rowell and Marriott (2007), pp. 113–15.

13 World Bank (1981).

14 Gran (1982).

15 *Ibid.*

16 OAU (1980).

17 Final Act of Lagos (April 1980), paragraph II.A; included as Annex I in *ibid.*, pp. 98–100.

18 If the apparent association of commodity dependence with low indices in these fields holds, as suggested above, this could be an underlying reason for the deterioration in the poorest countries' commodity export positions.

19 World Bank (1986), p. 64.

20 UNCTAD (2003a), Tables 3.13.3 (p. 158), 3.13.4 (p. 161), 3.14.3 (p. 175) and 3.14.4 (p. 177). The tables are available online at «www.r0.unctad. org/infocomm/comm_docs/cybframes.htm» (as of November 2007).

21 See *ibid.*, Table A.2.

22 This turned out to be an unwise business decision, as in 2005 the accumulated high-price stocks affected the company's profits when the price fell (reported in the *Daily Record*, Baltimore, 23 March 2005; located at «findarticles.com/p/articles/mi_qn4183/is_20050323/ai_n13473 939» in November 2007).

23 Information from Nyapendi (2005), *New Vision* (2005), Paul (2003), Butler (2005), FAOSTAT Database, IRIN (2005) and *The Hindu Business Line* (2006).

24 Nissanke and Thorbecke (2007), p. 230.

25 Basic information is available from the International Copper Study Group at «www.icsg.org/Factbook/copper_world/production_consumption.htm» (August 2005).

26 «stats.unctad.org/Handbook/TableViewer/tableView.aspx», Table 4.2 (July 2007).

27 See, for example, Russell (2007) and other articles at «www.ft.com/angola».

28 Wallis (2007).

29 According to Sguazzin (2005), the planned mine at Ambatovy was projected

to generate sales of US$1.3 billion per year at 2005 prices. Madagascar exported goods worth $763 million in 2005 and $766 million in 2006 («stats.unctad.org/Handbook/TableViewer/tableView.aspx»).

30 UNCTAD (2002), p. 124. The mineral-exporting LDCs are identified as the Central African Republic, DR Congo, Guinea, Liberia, Niger, Sierra Leone and Zambia.

31 *Ibid.*, p. 126. UNCTAD listed 21 LDCs as agricultural exporters.

32 stats.unctad.org/Handbook/TableViewer/tableView.aspx, Table 3.2 (consulted in November 2007). Total world coffee exports were worth $15.6 billion in 1995 and $15.8 billion in 2005. Of these amounts, developing countries in Africa accounted for $2.16 billion (or 13.9 per cent) in 1995 and $1.16 billion (7.3 per cent) in 2005; and LDCs for $1.33 billion (8.6 per cent) and $868,000 (5.5 per cent) respectively.

33 UNCTAD (2004), p. 236.

34 UNCTAD (2002), Table 35, p. 147.

35 Imber *et al.* (2003), p. 19. For an extended account, see Kanji *et al.* (2004).

36 Dembele (2004), p. 3 of 5.

37 Berkman (2007), p. 167. The author, Steve Berkman, worked for the World Bank in 1983–95 and 1998–2002.

38 *Ibid.*, p. 174.

39 Chang (2007).

40 Shafaeddin (2006), p. 21.

41 Datuk Seri Rafidah Aziz, Minister for International Trade and Industry, interviewed on BBC Television's *Newsnight* programme in July 2005.

42 Quoted in Nolan (1995), pp. 173–4.

43 Leith (2005), p. 58. Leith's book gives a shrewd and detailed account of Botswana's development.

44 AERC (2007), p. 4 (emphasis added).

45 UNDP (2005).

46 For a thoughtful analysis of the double standards involved, see Christian Aid (2005).

47 Stein (2003), p. 171.

48 IMF (2005), Figures 1 and 2 and pp. 4–5. See also Tan (2005), section 4.3, p. 17.

49 Dembele (2004), p. 3 of 5.

50 *Ibid.*, p. 5 of 5.

3
Do the market's job for it

The commodity markets are booming, aren't they?

It may seem odd to write about falling commodity prices at a time when some of the commodity markets have been booming for several years. Oil prices have increased sharply, as have the prices of many metals and some other commodities, including, since 2006, some widely traded cereals such as wheat. Some commentators have called it a 'commodities supercycle';[1] we should all hope that it turns out to be so. However, anyone who follows the commodities trade knows that it is futile to make any firm predictions about prices. Unless you know what you are doing extremely well, speculating on those prices is one of the surest ways of losing money.

There was similar excited talk during the last big commodities boom in the mid- to late 1970s. However, that boom was followed by a steep decline in prices in the first half of the 1980s, as demand fell off during the biggest international recession for 50 years. At the time of writing it appears just as likely either that the boom will continue for quite a while yet, as demand for raw materials imports from China and elsewhere remains buoyant; or that there will be a repeat of 1981–5, as the 2007 credit crisis leads to a wider economic crisis which will rebound on commodities. By the end of 2007 there were already signs that the commodities boom was running out of steam, but it was too soon to reach any firm conclusions. However, of one thing we can be certain: the systems that determine commodity prices provide no guarantee that the boom will last, and there is no evidence that the long-term experience of price volatility and price decline has been overcome; on the contrary, the volatility of prices is confirmed in the very boom itself.

The present boom has affected different types of commodity to differing extents, and that differentiation appears to be greater than in previous booms. This was reflected in Table 3, which showed that most commodity prices were still substantially lower in real terms than they were during the 1970s boom.[2] The biggest real price rises since then have been for copper and crude petroleum (or oil): commodities which feed the industrial economy but are little produced in the poorest developing countries (with some exceptions such as Angola, Nigeria and Zambia). The boom in such prices means little for countries whose major export has been little affected by these trends (for example, tea in Kenya) or has experienced price movements for its own reasons, quite independently of any other markets (such as vanilla in Madagascar).

Interest in the commodities problem has slowly re-emerged since the start of the new millennium, when the prices of many primary commodities exported by developing countries collapsed to their lowest-ever levels in relation to other products. This had a devastating effect on dozens of countries, especially the poorest and those with the weakest development indicators. It became widely apparent that it was anomalous to continue to ignore this question. Here is the UN Conference on Trade and Development (UNCTAD) account of what declining prices had meant for the Least Developed Countries: 'The volume of commodity exports from LDCs increased by 43 per cent between 1986 and 1999. . . . But the value of LDC commodity exports increased by only 26 per cent over this period, and the purchasing power of commodity exports increased by only 3 per cent between 1986 and 1999.'[3] As we saw in Chapter 2, the poorest countries had to run ever faster in order to stay where they were: an increase of more than 40 per cent in the quantities they exported brought virtually no increase in what they could buy with the proceeds. The export orientation dogma had led them into a trap from which it still remains exceedingly difficult for them to extricate themselves.

In this context, the following points may be noted about particular commodities shown in Table 3:

- **Coffee**: This is the most important export commodity for developing countries and we can see that its real price has collapsed since the 1970s heyday of the International Coffee Agreement, the price stabilization clauses of which were abandoned in 1989.

- **Cocoa**: The cocoa price also collapsed after many years of oversupply, in large part the result of the fallacy of composition in the main cocoa-producing countries in Africa, which were subject to structural adjustment policies. It has been reported that in France in 1960, 20 per cent of the price of a chocolate bar paid for its cocoa bean content, but only 5 per cent in more recent years; this was a consequence of the decline in the cocoa bean's price.[4]

- **Wheat and maize**: The prices of widely traded cereals fell sharply over the period shown, the wheat price declining the least but still by nearly one-third in real terms. However, between 2006 and 2007 the wheat price doubled due to a decline in world stocks;[5] maize prices also increased due to a surge in demand for the crop as a source of bioethanol in the US.

- **Rice**: International rice prices fell by more than half in real terms. This is worrying for three reasons. With the exception of the US, all the leading rice-exporting countries are developing countries, led by Thailand, and the price fall indicates a sharp decline in their terms of trade for this commodity. Second, it affects all farmers who sell rice and goes some way to explaining rural poverty in many countries of Asia, where the towns and cities have prospered. However, rice imports in many poor countries have rapidly expanded, especially in parts of Africa. This was facilitated by the fall in the real price, which not only made it more difficult for farmers in an importing country to make a living from rice, but also made rice more attractive for consumers than traditional, local staple foods. We shall return to this point in Chapter 5.

- **Cotton**: Real cotton prices have fallen by even more than rice prices. This has been exhaustively analysed elsewhere in response to the inclusion of cotton in the negotiations on agriculture at the WTO's Doha Round.[6] There are two main reasons: competition from synthetic fibres and the very high subsidies paid to cotton farmers in the US and the EU, which mean they can undercut all other producers on the international market. Those worst affected are some very poor West African countries for which cotton is a leading export and source of rural employment, notably Benin, Burkina Faso, Chad and Mali.

- **Tropical log** prices have fallen less than those of most non-mineral commodities. Their supply is controlled by the limited quantity of trees in tropical forests, and the time required to remove them to the market. Their steadier prices have made it more rewarding to cut down forests and sell the logs than to export most agricultural crops.

- **Minerals and metals**: There have been much sharper increases in these prices than those for other commodities, in large part because of demand from industry and for infrastructure development in China. The pattern has been very uneven between one metal and another, however. The price of tin, for example, has never recovered since the breakdown of the International Tin Agreement in 1985. However, real iron ore prices have risen, partly because in the late 1970s they were weak due to a chronic oversupply at that time, and partly because the world market is now dominated by just three companies at a time of increased demand. The copper price has risen the furthest of all; it is always one of the most volatile and its recent price boom has been fuelled by speculation at least as much as by demand for physical metal.

- **Crude petroleum**: Over the 27 years covered, this price increased faster on average than any other shown, except copper. In 1977 and 1978 the price was relatively low but it rose sharply in 1979, the year of Iran's revolution. But even the real price increase of 52 per cent between 1977–9 and 2004–6 is quite modest in comparison with the 50 to 75 per cent collapses found among several other commodities, including some major exports of poor developing countries.

In general, the markets that have boomed the least are those on which the poorest countries depend the most, for example cotton and beverages such as coffee. Their markets have exhibited no more than a routine cyclical upturn: indeed, the coffee price is not merely below its last cyclical peak of 1997, but at the time of writing it had only just returned to the fairtrade movement's *floor* price of $1.26 per kg for the arabica variety, which was established in the mid-1990s to protect growers at times of severe market crisis.

In these circumstances, either a country's imports must decline or other foreign-currency receipts must increase. In recent years a typical outcome has been, in effect, to supplement the export of goods such as coffee, bananas and copper with the export of the country's own people. People move north from Central America to the United States, or from Africa in the hope of finding a livelihood in Europe; women from the Philippines travel to Hong Kong to work as maids, while men from Pakistan and India go to work in the oil economies of the Arabian Gulf, and Polish men go west to find work in Great Britain; men from Moldova go east to poorly paid jobs in Russia, while some of their country's women end up in Western Europe's sex trade. Many people pay large sums to exploitative middlemen to make these journeys, and some of them never even arrive. Some of the emigrants are doctors, lawyers, university teachers and nurses, trained in their own countries where they are badly needed, but able to earn much more in the rich world, even from menial work. This emigration drains their countries of people and talent, but at least when they do find jobs, most of them send some of their pay back to their families at home. In many countries, these remittances from citizens abroad have become a major source of foreign income, reportedly exceeding the value of exported goods in places as diverse as Albania, Haiti, Jamaica, the Lebanon, Serbia and Tonga. In Moldova, migrants' earnings reportedly contribute 38 per cent of national income.[7]

However, questions of foreign trade can seem remote from poor rural people and their livelihoods. The exact nature of the linkages between trade and rural incomes can be hard to trace, even where crops are grown for export, while the quantitative effects on employment and earnings can be still harder to estimate; but those linkages not only exist but are often of profound importance for prosperity. The commodities trade is the linchpin, for the simple reason that as long as a country mainly produces primary goods, it has to export some of them in order to pay for its imports. What it earns from commodities, and by extension how the commodity markets themselves operate, is of critical importance for the country's present and its future.

Problems in how commodity markets work

On the whole, commodity markets do not do their basic job of matching supply with demand via the price system with any degree of efficiency. A series of problems in the ways these markets work indirectly exacerbates poverty in the countries that rely on them for their exports. I will describe each of these problems in turn.

Unstable prices
In Chapter 2 we saw how vanilla prices have moved in recent years, rising from $20 per kg in 1999 to $450 per kg in 2004 and then falling back to $20–$25 per kg for even the best produce in 2006. Similar patterns are frequently found on commodity markets. The difference between the highest price in the cycle and the lowest is not always so high, but in small markets like that for vanilla this is not rare. And many countries, like Madagascar, rely on such narrow, specialized markets for a large part of their export income. Large and unpredictable swings in price can also be found in big global markets like the oil market. In this respect, the commodity markets are more like those in which assets are bought and sold, such as the share market and the housing market, than those for manufactured goods.

Three main reasons can be identified for the volatility of agricultural markets in particular.

(a) *Seasonality and unpredictability of crops.* Farmers throughout the world complain about the weather, and with good reason. Their output is subject to natural forces in a way that affects few other parts of the economy. Good weather can improve a crop, both in size and quality, while bad weather can destroy it. Production is also vulnerable to pests and diseases. None of these influences on supply can be safely predicted, and when they occur they can create sudden shortages or surpluses, with inevitable effects on price. But those effects can be paradoxical. For example, good weather creating a large crop can also depress prices because the market will be oversupplied.

(b) *Unresponsiveness of supply and demand to price changes.* Demand for many agricultural products is inelastic: this means it fails to alter very much in response to increases or decreases in the price which are caused by fluctuations in supply. There is, after all, only a certain amount of food that one person can eat. On the supply side, both for tree crops (such as cocoa, coffee, rubber and tea) and many minerals, several years are required between the planting of trees or planning of mines and the first output from them. The size of the investment together with this timelag means that supply also responds inflexibly to both increases and decreases in demand. Sometimes the new supply will appear just when demand takes a downturn, and it will therefore amplify the weakness of market conditions. These faulty mechanisms on both the supply and the demand sides result in sharp movements in price.

(c) *Speculation.* People can make money out of buying and selling goods whose prices are volatile, without having any use for the physical product itself. This is facilitated where there is 'futures' trading in a commodity. On a futures market, it is not goods available 'on the spot' that are mainly traded, but promises to supply them at some date in the future (usually at various intervals up to 18 or 21 months forward). Futures exchanges like to attract speculators since they provide extra income (or 'liquidity') for the market. The speculator (like any other participant in a futures market) only has to buy or sell a 'paper' contract and does not have to store the material themselves; nor do they have to put up more than a small proportion of the full price. Nor, in practice, do they have to deliver or take delivery on the contract: before it is due, they cancel it out with an opposing contract for the same volume for delivery on the same day (to buy if the original contract was to sell, and *vice versa*). They make or lose money from the differences in price between the buy and sell contracts. A speculator can make money even when a price is falling: they will sell for future delivery and cancel this with a buy contract at a later date. This is called 'selling short'. If their forecast of a price fall is correct, they will make a profit on the business.

However, it is not universally agreed what effect speculation has on prices. Some economists argue that it complements physical demand and therefore evens out price fluctuations which arise from the vagaries of supply and demand; but a common observation on the markets is that speculators tend to 'ride' with price trends, and so make prices move *further* in either direction. A balance between these conflicting views was struck in one authoritative book: 'On balance, there appears to be a consensus that in normal times, speculation stabilizes the market, whereas in times of large shortages or surpluses, it tends to accentuate the instability of the market.'[8] However, since the biggest problems on commodity markets arise just when there are large shortages or surpluses, this would suggest that the destabilizing effects of speculation are more serious overall than when it has a stabilizing effect. If this quotation is correct, speculation tends to exaggerate both upward price 'spikes' and downward troughs. Among those engaged in actual production and trade, this can lead to inappropriate investment decisions (and therefore exaggerated price fluctuations again in future years), as well as large windfall gains and arbitrary losses of income.

There is plenty of evidence that speculative funds have affected prices during the present commodities boom. Many commodity funds have been established, attracting investment from small investors and other sources, and the money has gone into futures trading and the shares of mining companies. This has amplified the price rises for some commodities for which there are futures exchanges, such as copper and wheat. When the boom is over, these funds will be withdrawn and investors will try their luck in other markets, such as bonds or works of art, and this will exaggerate the price decline that follows.

Commodity prices can be unstable both over short periods of a few weeks or months and over the length of the business cycle – usually about eight to ten years. Commodity markets are notorious for instability of both sorts, but different means are required to tackle them. Where a futures market exists, those with the capital and financial understanding to do so can guard against short-term price fluctuations by 'hedging' their forthcoming purchases or sales with matching future sales or purchases on paper. These are then redeemed when the time comes, so that any gain or loss in the price movement is countered by the futures trades. That, at any rate, is the theory of hedging. It is a form of insurance against adverse price movements, and the utility of futures markets in providing it should not be scorned. But while the basic principles are simple, the dividing line between a commercial hedging transaction and a speculative bet on the market is not as clear as one might think. To carry it out effectively requires fine judgements and it can lead to large losses if those judgements are wrong. Some developing countries' commodity export agencies have discovered that from hard experience (as indeed have some big trading houses in the world's leading financial centres).

In any case, hedging on futures markets can only take care of short-term price fluctuations, because these markets do not go further into the future than one-and-a-half or two years at most; until quite recently, the London Metal Exchange's contracts went only three months forward. However, it is medium-term fluctuations that can be the most devastating. Take, for example, Ethiopia's experience between 1997 and 2005. When coffee prices are high, Ethiopia gets about two-thirds of its export revenues from coffee; 1997 was one such year and its exports of unroasted, or 'green', coffee were worth $350 million. Four years later, when the international price had collapsed, they came to just $127 million, or 64 per cent less. Another four years on, the prices were recovering and Ethiopia's green coffee exports had nearly tripled again in value to $353 million.[9] How can a country with all of Ethiopia's difficulties be expected to handle such abrupt changes on its own? It makes any economic planning very perilous. The same question can be asked of Madagascar, faced in recent years with the extreme price volatility of vanilla, its biggest export; and of many other countries that regularly face similar predicaments.

Such commodity price shocks can have severe local effects as well as national ones. In 2002 the charity Oxfam quoted an Ethiopian coffee farmer who described some of the things he could no longer afford to buy because of the collapse in coffee prices. There were 12 members of his household, including three children who had stopped going to school because he could not afford their uniforms. Moreover, his children were showing signs of mal-nutrition. In consequence of the coffee price collapse there was a sharp fall in price of the grain that this farmer also produced, since coffee farmers and their workers had been among the main customers for grain; now they grew their own food because they could not afford to buy it on the market.[10]

One solution to these problems is to provide monetary compensation to poor countries that suffer such reverses in their export revenues. Compensatory finance of this sort has a history of more than 30 years. The biggest schemes have been the IMF's Compensatory Finance Facility and the Stabex programme which existed under the EU's former Lomé agreements with African, Caribbean and Pacific countries. However, these schemes have been bureaucratic, the money has been disbursed slowly and they have steadily become less generous over the years. This is not how they were originally foreseen. In 1973 a very simple idea was proposed: 'a compensatory financial arrangement under which all, or part, of the difference between actual prices and an agreed reference price would be made up to the exporting countries'.[11] This would be simple and automatic, it would make very limited administrative demands on either side, and the payments could be made just when needed. In 2003 a meeting convened by UNCTAD called on the European Commission and the IMF to design a simple compensatory finance system that would be quick-disbursing and easier to use than the previous ones, with a mechanism to pass the funds through to actual producers and consumers.[12] It could operate with the simple arrangement proposed in 1972.

Long-term tendency of prices to decline
It has long been argued that commodity prices tend to decline in real terms over a long period, and this has been amply borne out since the 1980s. However, the great economist J. M. Keynes wrote:

> Proper economic prices should be fixed not at the lowest possible level, but at the level sufficient to provide producers with proper nutritional and other standards in the conditions in which they live … and it is in the interests of all producers alike that the price of a commodity should not be depressed below this level, and *consumers are not entitled to expect that it should.*[13]

But the prices received not long ago by the Ethiopian coffee farmer did fall below that level, and likewise for vast numbers of other people around the world. The export orientation policies imposed under structural adjustment exaggerated the danger.

Three main reasons can be identified for the falls in real prices over recent decades:

(a) *Oversupply*. Many of the markets for tropical export commodities became chronically oversupplied. For example, world production of cocoa exceeded consumption by more than 20 per cent in three separate years in the 1990s, and the oversupply of coffee was 18 per cent in 2000, when the coffee price collapsed. We saw in Chapter 2 how this tendency was linked with the export orientation strategy advocated by the World Bank and other donors, and the fallacy of composition which was built into it. The consequence was a severe weakening of export farmers' commercial position on many vital markets. According to UNCTAD in 2002, 'World Bank research has shown that this adding-up problem

(or fallacy of composition) affects a number of agricultural commodities, notably bananas, cocoa, coffee, cotton, tea and tobacco..
.. These commodities constituted 42 per cent of the total non-fuel
primary commodity exports of LDCs in 1997–9.'[14]

(b) *Prebisch and Singer.* Hans Singer and Raúl Prebisch, two of the
pioneers of development economics, made their names
concurrently in 1950 with papers that observed and explained a
long-term tendency of commodity prices to decline in relation to
those of manufactured goods. They said there was a structural
reason for this, since demand for manufactures was more elastic
(and so could expand more rapidly and responsively) than that for
commodities. Much the same case was made in less technical
language by Adam Smith nearly two centuries earlier: 'The desire
of food is limited in every man by the narrow capacity of the
human stomach; but the desire of the conveniences and ornaments
of building, dress, equipage and household furniture, seems to have
no limit or certain boundary.'[15] Indeed, that is the basis on which
capitalism has developed ever since Smith's time.

(c) *Subsidies.* On certain markets, declining prices are explained by
the impact of subsidies given to Northern farmers. This is most
problematic for those export commodities that are produced and
exported by both developed and developing countries. Some of
them (such as wheat) are also exported to developing countries,
and the subsidies permit their producers to undercut the domestic
prices in the importing country. Other subsidized crops are
produced in the North in competition with developing countries'
exports to third countries, with a similar effect on world prices. A
well-known example of this lies in the high US and EU subsidies for
cotton, which have indirectly reduced the earnings of cotton
farmers in West Africa.

Buyer power
It is not only declining prices at the point of international trade but
the farmers' declining share of final retail prices which led to crisis.

This is the third price issue that needs to be addressed. It is a worldwide problem, which British farmers also complain about, and for much the same reason. The bargaining power of those near the consumer end of agricultural supply chains has increased, enabling supermarkets and others to force down their own purchase prices and leave any excess stocks to hang over at the producers' end of the chain. This in turn has forced down the prices received by the producers themselves. It is necessary to move economic power further back in the chain towards the producers, but what instruments can be used to achieve this? That will be discussed in more detail in the next chapter.

While commodity price volatility has been well-known for a long time, and the long-term real decline of commodity prices was first suggested nearly 60 years ago, this third problem is a more recent development superimposed on the other two. It arises from excessive concentration at key trading points along the supply chain. For example, there are just five people who purchase imported flowers for British supermarkets, and flowers are now an important export product for some countries, such as Kenya and Colombia. This trend started some time ago, but it has only recently gained worldwide significance. More than 30 years ago, during the 1970s price boom, it was reported in the US that:

> Even with an investment of several hundred thousand dollars, and hundreds of thousands of acres, the grain farmer is caught between the banks and the corporations that provide capital inputs on one end, and the grain monopolies on the other.... It is not the farmer who benefits from higher prices. [US] food prices have risen 43 per cent since 1952, but the price the farmer receives for his production has increased only 6 per cent.[16]

Where developing countries' exports are concerned, a similar phenomenon can be seen in the British coffee market, in which Nestlé has enjoyed more than a 50 per cent market share through its Nescafé brand. Over the last two coffee price cycles there was a sharp increase in the difference between the prices charged for coffee in British shops and those of the green coffee beans that are traded and priced internationally. Between the last cyclical price

Table 5 Commodity-dependent developing countries (2003—5)* grouped by the character of trade access to the US and EU of their leading commodity export

Leading export commodity	Country	Population 2004 (millions)	% of exports from leading commodity, 2005 unless stated	Human development ranking, 2004	GDP per capita, US$ (PPP) 2004
1 Preferential trade access (for some developing countries)					
Bananas	St Vincent	0.1	26	88	6,398
Beef	Uruguay	3.4	22	43	9,421
Sugar	Guyana	0.8	28	103	4,439
2 Support for EU or US producers, without preferential access for the South					
Cotton	Burkina Faso	12.8	59 (2004)	174	1,113
	Benin	8.2	29	163	1,091
Fish	Eritrea	4.2	21 (2003)	157	977
	Namibia	2.0	24 (2003)	125	7,418
	Panama	3.2	31	58	7,278
	Seychelles	0.1	57	47	16,652
Fruit juices	Belize	0.3	26	95	6,747
	Cook Islands	<0.1	32 (2004)	—	—
Milk	Maldives	0.3	43	98	—
Soya beans	Paraguay	6.0	37	91	4,813
Tobacco	Malawi	12.6	53	166	646
	Zimbabwe	12.9	21 (2004)	151	2,065
3 Tropical crops sold on free markets					
Cocoa	São Tomé & Principe	0.2	88 (2003)	122	—
	Côte d'Ivoire	17.9	31	164	1,551
	Ghana	21.7	36	136	2,240
Coffee	Burundi	7.3	84	169	677
	Ethiopia	75.6	40	170	756
	Uganda	27.8	18	145	1,478
	Rwanda	8.9	42	158	1,263
	Sierra Leone	5.3	73 (2002)	176	561
	Honduras	7.0	20	117	2,876
	Nicaragua	5.4	16	112	3,634
Tea	Kenya	33.5	17	152	1,140
Vanilla	Madagascar	18.1	14 (2004)	143	857

Table 5 cont.

Leading export commodity	Country	Population 2004 (millions)	% of exports from leading commodity, 2005 unless stated	Human development ranking, 2004	GDP per capita, US$ (PPP) 2004
4 Metals and minerals					
Aluminium	Mozambique	19.4	45 (2002)	168	1,237
Bauxite & alumina	Guinea	9.2	36 (2002)	160	2,180
Cement & lime	Togo	6.0	17	147	1,536
Copper	Mongolia	2.6	31	116	2,056
Gold	Kyrgyzstan	5.2	34	110	1,935
	Mali	13.1	60 (2001)	175	998
	Peru	27.6	19	82	5,678
	Tanzania	37.6	33	162	674
Iron ore	New Caledonia	0.2	63	—	—
Nickel ore	Cuba	11.2	37	50	—
Pearls & precious stones	Botswana	1.8	67	131	9,945
	French Polynesia	0.3	61	—	—
	Central African Rep.	4.0	31	172	1,094
	Armenia	3.0	28	80	4,101
Precious metal ores	Papua-New Guinea	5.8	29 (2003)	139	2,543
Uranium ore	Niger	13.5	32 (2003)	177	779

* As defined by Gibbon (2007), p. 6.
Sources: FAO («faostat.fao.org/site/336/default.aspx»), Gibbon (2007); International Trade Centre («www.intracen.org/menus/countries.htm»), UNCTAD («stats.unctad.org/handbook/ Report Folders/ReportFolders.aspx»), UNDP («hdr.undp.org/en/reports/global/hdr2006»), CIA World Fact Book

peak in May 1997 and the ensuing trough in September 2001, the average international price fell from 180.44 US cents per pound to 41.17 c/lb (as measured by the ICO's composite indicator). On the British retail market, however, the average price declined only from 1,607.80 c/lb at its (rather delayed) peak in April 1998 to 1,154.96 c/lb at the trough in February 2002. In the present upturn, the highest point for the international average price at the time of writing was in September 2007, when it rose to 113.20 c/lb, some 37 per cent below its 1997 peak. But by December 2006, the average retail price in the UK was already 1,781.61 c/lb, nearly eleven per cent *above* its 1998 peak. From peak to peak, it therefore rose from 8.9 times the international price in 1997–8 to 15.7 times the international price in 2006–7. There was a similar development between the cyclical lows of 1992–3 and 2001.[17]

Interestingly, it is the most freely operating (and therefore more volatile) markets that tend to be linked with the very poorest countries, as can be seen in Table 5. Based on a recent study,[18] it shows the countries in which non-oil commodities account for at least half of merchandise exports, in four groups according to the terms on which their main commodity are exported. The four categories of commodities are:

1 Three agricultural commodities in which a group of countries have had preferential access to the EU's market with import quotas. They are bananas, beef and sugar (although in bananas and sugar the quotas are being abandoned under pressure from the WTO).

2 Commodities produced in both tropical and temperate (or Mediterranean) climates, in which the EU and the US give their farmers significant public support or protection, without providing any countervailing advantage to developing countries' exports in the form of quotas or guaranteed import prices. These commodities are cotton, fish, fruit juices, milk, soya and tobacco.

3 Tropical crops in which the international market now operates

almost entirely freely. Included here are the main tropical beverages (coffee, cocoa and tea) and vanilla. For climatic reasons, none of these commodities can be produced in either the EU or the US.
4 Metals and minerals.

In Table 5, it is noticeable that the countries in Group 1 are better off for both human development and GDP *per capita* than the others, with the partial exception of those that depend on fish exports. There are only three countries in Group 1 here, but the same was found even more clearly in a previous exercise along similar lines in 2004, which included six banana-exporting and nine sugar-exporting countries.[19] And those that have long enjoyed large import quotas in the EU tend to be very small countries. The countries in Group 3, which rely on free export markets, are much poorer than those in Group 1 and they include the three countries that are most dependent on a single non-oil commodity (Burundi, São Tomé & Principe and Sierra Leone); country groups 2 and 4 are somewhere between groups 1 and 3 for prosperity and human development. In line with our observations in Chapter 1, nearly all the 43 countries in this list are small: Ethiopia has by far the largest population among them. But those that depend on free agricultural markets tend to have larger populations than the others.

The implication is that few commodity-specific concessions are made to those countries that appear to be most in need of them. Those in greatest poverty depend on minerals or other commodities that are traded in almost completely free markets or, in a few cases, those where they compete with heavily subsidized Northern farmers. From the point of view of poverty reduction, such countries deserve privileges but have not received them; or if they did exist, as in the former system of coffee export quotas, they were abandoned some time ago. This is in contrast to the generous, commodity-specific support accorded to countries in Group 1, from which imports to the EU have been managed under quotas for many years.

Under the EU's particularly generous ACP (Africa, Caribbean and Pacific) Sugar Protocol, which has hitherto guaranteed prices at three times the world market's levels, the five countries that have received the lion's share of import quotas have a combined population of only 6.4 million people (in order of quota size: Mauritius, Fiji, Guyana, Jamaica and Swaziland). But this preferential market access has depressed sugar prices for poorer and bigger countries that either have surpluses for export, such as Mozambique, or large domestic markets, such as Bangladesh – a similar price effect to that of EU and US subsidies on cotton and tobacco. The quota arrangements have clearly benefited the countries that received them, giving assured access to an important export market and so enabling them to plan their development, as is virtually impossible for a country in Mozambique's or Ethiopia's position. Indeed Mauritius, the recipient of by far the largest EU sugar quota, is often held up as a model of successful development; Barbados, a country of 300,000 people which also used to have a sizeable quota, is now as prosperous as such EU member states as the Czech Republic, Hungary and Malta. We shall see that comparable benefits also arose when export quotas governed the coffee market for 25 years from 1964 to 1989. It is hard to escape the conclusion that managed trade of this sort does more for development than global free markets do.

Breaking with tradition

So-called non-traditional commodities are frequently proposed as the solution to these problems. The concept is wide and diverse, and not subject to precise definition. It has been used by various authors to cover many different things. It generally excludes staple foods and products sold in well-established, large-scale North–South markets, such as coffee, cocoa, bananas, tobacco and jute, but it can refer to almost any commodity that has not in the past been an important export in a particular country or region. Indeed, an export commodity that is traditional in one country is often classed as non-traditional in another. Thus, in the example discussed in Chapter 2, vanilla was a non-traditional commodity in Uganda and Papua-New Guinea but a traditional one in Madagascar and Indonesia. But the market's characteristics remained the same, no matter where the spice was grown.

As part of a drive to diversify narrowly based economies, non-traditional commodities should in principle be desirable. Chosen as a means to gain extra export income, they tend to be in markets that are seen as expanding with good income opportunities for the future. A current example would be crops from which biofuels can be produced, such as palm oil, sugar cane and soya. Other popular ones are fish, other seafood and horticultural products (fresh fruit, vegetables and cut flowers). There is evidence of a widespread and even concerted push to build new infrastructure for trade in such commodities, especially in airfreight (new and expanded airports) and the refrigerated 'cold chain' (or 'chill chain') required in the transport of perishable products. So-called airport-aligned agricultural export zones are being established in fertile land which is designated to grow vegetables, fruit and flowers for export. These are comparable to the maritime industrial export processing zones which were pioneered in Singapore and played an important role in the early stages of China's industrial expansion. The following developments have been identified, among others:

> Developments of chill-chain linkages from airport aligned agricultural export zones ... to airport perishable centres are underway around many airports in many countries including South Africa, Tanzania, India, Gambia and adjacent to Colombo Airport in Sri Lanka. An outbound airborne chill-chain is developing in other countries with widespread malnutrition and hunger, such as Bangladesh, Pakistan, Nepal and Ethiopia.[20]

It is further pointed out that:

> The food air freight trade flow is largely, but not exclusively, perishable food from poorer countries to wealthier countries, with a strong relationship between high average per capita income and perishable imports shown clearly by the Cool Chain Association and estimates that 80% of Africa's air freight exports are perishables. The south feeds the north and the industry literature often refers to 'supplying' and 'consuming' countries.[21]

However, non-traditional commodities frequently provide a lot less than is promised. They do not escape the fallacy of composition and other weaknesses of commodity markets. The dangers may even be greater precisely because many of them are perishable, with deliveries required quickly and at short notice, which requires considerable logistical and managerial expertise; and they are not sold in great quantities or in bulk but go to narrow, specialized markets that can be overwhelmed easily by additional supply. Nearly all of them are traded on what are termed 'free' international markets, in reality forming part of vertically integrated supply chains controlled by Northern corporate buyers.

African countries in particular have been urged to produce fresh vegetables for export to rich countries, on the grounds that they are of higher value and offer greater financial margins than their traditional agricultural exports. It has been argued that

> The value chains of horticulture exports in Kenya ... show that the growth of labour intensive exports does create employment opportunities, particularly for low income women and migrants.... However, the requirements of global value chains mean that these jobs often demand a high degree of labour flexibility, long hours of work, and poor working conditions, making workers vulnerable both in terms of employment security and income.[22]

But, as seen in Table 6, over the years in which fresh vegetable exports have been promoted in sub-Saharan Africa (SSA), it is only Kenya's trade accounts that have actually benefited from them. Table 6 shows that the total value of vegetable exports from SSA countries increased by US$92 million (38 per cent) between 1990 and 2005, but their vegetable imports increased by $295 million, leading the deficit of imports against exports to nearly quadruple in value; the total volume of exports actually fell by 5,000 tons. Kenya meanwhile accounted for the whole increase in export value, with $13 million to spare. Even there, export horticulture has been criticized for providing decreasing benefits for smallholders as the exports have become concentrated in the hands of a few large producers, while they take up land and large amounts of water from

Table 6 Vegetable trade in sub-Saharan Africa, 1990 and 2005

Country	Year	Production ('000 metric tons)	Imports ('000 metric tons)	Imports (value in US$'000)	Exports ('000 metric tons)	Exports (value in US$'000)	Export surplus (+) or deficit (−) in US$'000*
Benin	1990	215	15	4,487	<1	154	−4,332
	2005	285	189	40,881	1	567	−40,314
Ghana	1990	399	6	3,259	4	1,301	−1,958
	2005	718	520	91,708	13	14,551	−77,157
Kenya	1990	1,200	11	1,668	53	44,731	+43,062
	2005	1,822	28	6,394	96	149,398	+143,004
Niger	1990	364	13	3,159	131	59,112	+55,953
	2005	793	22	5,050	58	15,002	+9,952
Nigeria	1990	4,668	109	66,764	2	1,256	−65,508
	2005	9,424	106	37,829	8	1,993	−35,836
South Africa	1990	1,983	47	22,768	127	66,793	+44,025
	2005	2,246	112	40,489	101	66,481	+25,992
SSA (total)	1990	17,877	817	317,171	472	241,251	−73,448
	2005	27,577	2,470	612,402	467	332,820	−276,943
Morocco	1990	3,033	3	1,801	346	178,392	+176,592
	2005	4,792	80	16,608	620	349,023	+332,415

* The figures might not add up, because of rounding.
Source: FAOSTAT Database, «faostat.fao.org/site/336/DesktopDefault.aspx?PageID=336», October 2007.

other agricultural uses. These data suggest that, far from being a universally replicable form of export activity, vegetable exports to developed countries should be seen as a narrow, specialized market, in which Kenya has the lion's share in sub-Saharan Africa, just as Madagascar does for vanilla and Zanzibar does for cloves.

The trade in horticultural commodities has been analysed extensively elsewhere, and found to be 'very concentrated with approximately two thirds of developing country exports accounted for by eight countries', and with no LDCs among the leading exporters.[23] This is well supported by the figures in Table 6, which show Morocco's export *surplus* in 2005 to have been worth as much as *all* of SSA's vegetable exports. It appears therefore to be a feasible option for a middle-income country that is quite close to European markets. But at the bottom end of the income scale, we see that from 1990 Niger's vegetable exports fell by three-quarters to just $15 million in 2005; and this was evidently not because of the food emergency that year in Niger, as its exports in 2000 were even lower at $13.7 million.[24] This may in part have been because of increasing domestic demand in Niger, since vegetable production there more than doubled. But output also doubled in Nigeria, which had been the leading market for Niger's most important vegetable exports, green beans and onions.

In fact Nigeria accounted for nearly half of SSA's vegetable production increase, enabling it to reduce its deficit in vegetable trade by nearly half. Some other lessons from Nigeria's food production performance will be discussed in Chapter 5. Here it offers a stark contrast with Ghana, where vegetable imports ballooned to $92 million as a consequence of reducing its import tariffs under trade liberalization; that was more than twice the imports of any other African country.

Many maritime countries have also been persuaded to permit large-scale fishing fleets (many of them from the EU) to fish in their offshore waters, in order to provide export income. There has also been expansion in some inland fisheries, for example in Lake Victoria in East Africa. Much of the fish and seafood is airfreighted out, as just described. But in consequence in many places, particularly along the West African coast, there are no longer enough fish to make traditional *inshore* fisheries worthwhile; and not only have the people who were engaged in fishing lost their livelihoods, but national supplies of protein have been reduced and other sources of protein have had to be found. In some cases this was 'bushmeat' (wild animals). One study found that the species affected included large carnivores such as lions, leopards and hyenas; primates including colobus and mona monkeys; and herbivores such as hippopotami, giant hogs and bongo antelopes.[25]

Can we manage?

Taken together, the evidence of the commodity markets indicates that in general they *fail* in their tasks. The premise of the Berg Report in 1981, and the World Bank's campaign to 'get the prices right' which followed it, was that government measures such as border tariffs and marketing boards distort market outcomes, and therefore the efficiency of trade. But the combination of volatile prices, inadequate responses of supply and demand to price signals, and market concentration at certain points on the supply chain means that *the commodity markets themselves severely distort the outcomes of trade and the distribution of its benefits.*

No doubt as a response to the price crisis in the first years of the new millennium, there is renewed interest in developing countries in the problems of commodity prices. If free markets cannot ensure that supply matches demand and prices are reasonably stable and remunerative enough to provide producers with proper nutrition (as Keynes cautioned), something else will have to do so on their behalf. But how can it be done? A traditional, but currently unfashionable, answer in many cases lies in managed trade, including what is called public supply management. Supply management (SM) is any concerted technique that reduces the supplies in a market, or increases them, in order to influence price movements. It is in fact a regular part of the commodities trade and is generally pursued by whoever is in a dominant position on a given market. On any large international market, supplies are likely to be effectively controlled by somebody at some point along the supply chain.

Supply management can take many forms, and the best form for any market can only be discovered with reference to that market. It is not always easy to implement, but it has worked successfully in producers' interests over long periods on several markets: for example, in the international tea market (1933–55), in coffee (1964–89) and on five domestic agricultural markets in Canada to this day. Its introduction alone can have a dramatic effect on prices. The International Tea Agreement of 1933 is little remembered outside the tea trade, but the reduction in exports and the imposition of export quotas on tea producers that it introduced led to an immediate increase in prices, which rose by 50 per cent between 1932 and 1937.[26] Some years later, events on the coffee market were even more dramatic:

> In November 1940 the Inter-American Coffee Agreement was signed between the US and all Latin American producing countries. It inaugurated a system of export quotas for the North American market and thus ended the previous fierce competition among producing countries.... During the six months following the signing of the Agreement, prices soared by 60 per cent.[27]

Before the 1990s formal international commodity agreements (ICAs) operated on several markets, while corporate purchasers on modern agricultural markets use a commercial variant called supply chain management. Commercial forms of SM have also included the De Beers company's control of diamond distribution and the control of prices by aluminium and nickel transnational corporations (TNCs) until the 1980s. The aluminium system was extremely successful for the first 90 years in which that metal was traded; it benefited consumers and the producing companies by keeping aluminium prices stable and relatively low.[28]

Those examples all worked quite differently from each other: that is no accident, as every commodity market operates in its own way. Mechanisms have been used either to limit supplies in order to keep prices up or to manipulate supplies with a view to evening out price fluctuations. Many different means have been used to achieve this, by a variety of actors – some of them purely commercial, others representing farmers' interests, still others based in groups of producer states (such as OPEC on the oil market), and by producing and consuming countries operating in concert in the ICAs.

Innovative methods of supply management should now be investigated urgently market by market. These systems should be introduced or reintroduced wherever they are found to be feasible, with the support of sufficient finance from international institutions to ensure their success. While there may be some markets where something like the old ICAs will provide the best mechanism available, there are others where other methods of supply management will be more suitable.

This would respond to the renewed interest now shown by several developing countries which are in strong positions on certain commodity markets. For example, in May 2005 a new government in Ecuador (which exports more bananas than any other country) signed a decree to regulate the volume of bananas leaving the country.[29] Two months later, Malaysia and Indonesia announced a bilateral plan to cooperate on the palm oil, rubber, cocoa, timber and other markets in order to ensure price stability and eliminate the undercutting of their positions by others. 'Farmers of both countries are always on the receiving end when prices drop', the Malaysian commodities minister was reported as saying. These countries are the two leading producers of palm oil and the second and third producers of natural rubber.[30] On the world tea market, discussions have been reported involving all four leading tea producers, China, India, Kenya and Sri Lanka. According to an Indian newspaper, *The Telegraph*, India and China both favoured the proposal.[31]

Kenya is also one of the drivers of an initiative at the WTO to affirm the right of exporting countries to cooperate on commodity markets. In June 2006 the African Group at the WTO[32] called, among other things, for a legal instrument that would clearly authorize joint actions by producing countries to control overproduction or restrict exports on agricultural commodity markets, with the aim of achieving stable and remunerative prices. They would be permitted to do this either unilaterally or jointly with consuming countries. The proposal called for technical and financial support for such arrangements, including the compensation of farmers for losses of income in the period immediately after the adoption of supply management. This proposal was later endorsed by the Group of 90 countries, a collective group comprising all the WTO's developing country members – in other words, the great majority of the world's nations and people.

The instruments used to manage supplies at different times have included the manipulation of public or private stocks, both import and export quotas, tariffs, TNCs' controls over their own production and distribution systems, and tight commercial control over outsourced agricultural production. This last is referred to as supply chain management. Under it, commercial purchasers manage their own intakes in their commercial interests in order to purchase only as much as they can later sell at a given price level. This means that in the case of oversupply the surplus stocks will accumulate nearer the producers' end of the chain. By these means purchasers can force down their purchase prices at the expense of farms, plantations and agricultural employees. Modern stock-control processes make it possible to fine-tune the quantities purchased even more closely than before. In consequence, as has been pointed out, 'Risk and cost are passed down the supply chain to those most vulnerable, such as developing country farmers, and women or migrant and temporary workers. . . . Employment becomes more precarious.'[33] That sort of commercial, buyer-driven SM urgently needs to be counterbalanced in the interests of development and poverty reduction.

More widely, supplies can be managed with a view to either raising or lowering the price level, and both on national and international markets. There are methods that push supplies up (subsidies to domestic producers, import tariffs), cut them back (production or export quotas), or can do either at different times with the aim of reducing price volatility (a buffer stock or variations in quotas). The European Community's Common Agricultural Policy between the 1960s and 1980s, with its system of high guaranteed prices for farmers, intervention stocks and high external tariffs, is an example of supply management that kept prices high and *expanded* farm output (although at the cost of European consumers and taxpayers).

Figure 1 gives examples of supply management, both currently and historically, on a variety of agricultural and mineral markets. It shows which agent was in control of the process, what techniques they used, and on the horizontal axis whether they represented a private and commercial or a public or social interest. The vertical axis shows at what point that agent was on the supply chain

Figure 1 Types of commodity supply management (limited supply)

Who's in control?		State or socialized			Corporate		
		Commodity	Organization	Method	Commodity	Company/ies	Method
Producers/exporters	Monopoly control				Diamonds	De Beers (Central Selling Organization)	Sales control and stocking
	Oligopoly or cartel	Cereals (since 1992)	EU	Limits to sown area (set-aside)	Aluminium, nickel (in the past)	Alcan etc. INCO etc.	Vertical integration; production control and stocking
		Chickens, milk	Canadian farm co-ops	Production quotas			
		Oil	OPEC				
Producer-consumer agreement		Coffee (before 1989)	ICO	Export quotas			
		Tin (before 1985)	ITC	Buffer stock			
Consumers/importers	Oligopsony	Bananas	EU	Import quotas	Bananas	Dole etc.	Vertical integration; production control
					Coffee	Nestlé, Kraft etc.	Purchase control, supply chain management
					Other foods	Supermarkets	

between producers and final consumers. It can be seen that, with time, supplies have come to be managed from points further to the right and further down the chart, that is, by private and commercial rather than public or social interests, and nearer the consumer's end of the supply chain.

When people refer to supply management in relation to development, they usually have in mind the ICAs that existed at various times between the 1930s and the 1990s. They were drawn up between all the main producing and consuming countries of a commodity. Not all of them involved developing countries (for example, the International Wheat Agreement), but the ICAs are most closely associated with tropical export crops such as tea, coffee, cocoa and rubber, and metals like tin. Two of the most famous were the International Tin Agreement, which lasted from 1956 until 1985 (with precursors going back to the 1930s), and the International Coffee Agreement, the market intervention clauses of which operated from 1964 to 1989. The ICAs functioned by intervening in the market to keep prices within a predetermined band, considered to be the trend price for the commodity in question. Establishing an ICA required protracted negotiations between the principal countries on both sides of the market. However, the method does not have to be so formal. Most private companies make their pricing and production decisions according to commercial judgements rather than such hard-and-fast rules. The people running any revived systems could be given more operating flexibility, like their commercial counterparts.

The former ICAs were also unusual in that they were based on cooperation between countries on both the consumer and producer sides of a market. This was both a strength and a weakness: a strength in that once agreement is struck it is more likely to prove effective, but a weakness in that it can take longer to reach agreement, the formalities can be cumbersome, and powerful players on either side can wreck the agreement by pulling out. A further weakness lay, ironically, in the ICAs' one-size-fits-all nature, since they all used the same format requiring negotiation between the principal countries on both sides of the market and a mechanism of either export quotas or buffer stocks. This is the very fault of which structural adjustment has routinely been accused. But OPEC does not follow this pattern as it has never even included all the leading oil exporters, let alone the importing countries, and yet it has been successful in its own terms over many years.

Bit by bit during the 1980s and 1990s, as the ICAs came up for renewal, they found that either they had to abandon their market intervention clauses or the US withdrew. In the case of the coffee agreement – perhaps the most important of them all – both happened. The International Coffee Organization (ICO) still exists as a forum for countries involved in the coffee trade, but since the 1989 Agreement it has lacked the 'economic clauses' which regulated supplies by means of export quotas. Since then coffee prices have remained low at the point of farm sale and also in international trade, but the roasters have continued to make large profits[34] as retail prices in most of the big markets have steadily risen. The proposal for non-corporate management of supplies is no more than an attempt to correct for the serious power imbalances that arise from high present-day levels of market concentration, and the corporate commercial SM systems that result.

There were two reasons why the ICAs collapsed when they did. One is that the Reagan administration in the US withdrew its support from anything that smacked of market intervention in favour of poor countries. This was a political reason, not an inherent 'failure' in the agreements themselves, and it matched in international trade institutions the work done in developing countries' domestic policy by structural adjustment and IMF loan conditions. However, the second reason lay in the sharp economic recession of the early 1980s, which forced prices down and built up stocks on commodity markets. This smashed an apparently robust ICA, the International Tin Agreement, because it took so much metal off the market to keep the price up that its buffer stock ran out of funds; but it also destroyed even the previously solid pricing arrangement between the major aluminium producers.

There is a long history of unilateral forms of supply management by commodity-exporting countries. Several of them were established in the 1970s in imitation of OPEC, although with mixed success. More recent was the Association of Coffee Producing Countries, set up by leading Latin American producers after the cessation of the ICO's export quotas. OPEC has been relatively successful over a long period in an export industry that is dominated by powerful TNCs. The producer governments have retained substantial influence over production decisions. Oil is a scarce resource, and an agreement that limits supplies in the short term should allow producers to benefit from higher prices in the future, when oil starts to run out. This has added a strong incentive to stick to the agreement. However, while oil prices are high at present, OPEC has not managed to keep them up continuously since its first price hike in 1973. Indeed, UNCTAD's figures show that the crude oil price has been one of the more unstable commodity prices since the 1970s.[35] Nevertheless, throughout this period OPEC has remained influential; few other groups of commodity-producing countries can claim the same.

And there are many advantages in a producer-led approach. It can build effectively on solidarity where it exists. Agreement is more easily reached than over an ICA, since in principle all the members will have a common interest. In the right market, it can enable producers to exert those interests much more effectively. The success of such an initiative would depend greatly on the number of exporting countries that joined it and the extent to which other participants in the market could be prevented from undermining it with expanded exports from non-member countries.

However, the requirements for supply management of any form to succeed are quite exacting and they will not be met in all cases. SM is partly a technical process, using certain tools to control the amounts supplied on a market, and partly an instrument of market power. In order for it to succeed, the technical and political requirements both need to be satisfied. First, let us consider the technical problems. On the international commodity markets, publicly run supply management has worked where there is a global market with a common pricing system and a single set of market institutions. Many markets have been global for decades, and in some cases for centuries: large markets like oil, coffee and copper as well as tin, palm oil and rubber, and small, specialized ones like vanilla, cloves and tungsten. But not all of them are, even now.

A second issue is whether you want to stabilize prices or push them up. In designing a supply management scheme it is necessary to be clearsighted about this. UNCTAD's aim in the 1970s was to achieve commodity prices that would be at once 'stable and remunerative'. The one that was most lauded at the time, the International Tin Agreement, appeared to achieve both until it collapsed in 1985. Any supply management system should decide at the outset which of the two it mainly wants to achieve. Any scheme can also come under severe, unpredictable strain at times, and provisions to accommodate that strain should be built in. The impact of the severe early 1980s recession on commodity supply management was not foreseen, but in future the possibility of such strains could be built into any agreement with something akin to a *force majeure* provision.

Among advocates of international supply management, there is a consensus now that limits on actual production should be used where possible. That is one of the reasons for OPEC's success – admittedly in a market in which supplies can literally be turned on and off, unlike most commodities. The coffee agreement's export quotas were abandoned in 1989 partly because they were more easily evaded than effectively monitored production quotas would be. On the other hand, import and export quotas have worked to good developmental effect in other forms of managed trade, as we saw in the case of sugar.

While there are serious technical challenges, the problems in supply management are just as often political, and they should be addressed squarely as such. One condition of success is the existence of a dedicated core of countries (or companies, in a commercial cartel) which feel solidarity with each other on other grounds. This clearly applies to the Middle Eastern countries in OPEC and it was also true of Indonesia, Malaysia and Thailand in the tin agreement. However, solidarity in the coffee market is more elusive because of the large number and diversity of the exporting countries, while an attempt by copper-producing developing countries to intervene in the market in the 1960s got almost nowhere because the countries concerned were too diverse.

All of the above suggests that supply management will not work on every market, and certainly not by the same means on every one. But when you look at what has happened to coffee prices since the market was liberalized with the end of export quotas in 1989, it seems that the liberalization cure can be much worse than the 'disease'.

Notes

1   See, for example, Brown, Crawford and Gibson (2008), p. 7.
2   The list of commodities is the same as in a table published by UNCTAD in 2006. See UNCTAD (2006b), Table 1.A1, p. 18.
3   UNCTAD (2002), Part 2, Chapter 4, p. 139.
4   UNCTAD and Common Fund (2004), pp. 8–9.
5   Blas (2007).

6   Many articles can be found by typing 'WTO cotton' into a general web search engine.

7   Lapper (2007), citing the World Bank as source.

8   MacBean and Nguyen (1987), p. 132.

9   «faostat.fao.org/site/336/default.aspx» (November 2007).

10 See Oxfam International (2002), p. 10.

11 Maizels (1973), p. 48. At the time, Alf Maizels was the deputy director of UNCTAD's Commodities Division.

12 UNCTAD (2003d), pp. 4–5 and 10.

13 Keynes (1946); emphasis added.

14 UNCTAD (2002), p. 162, which cites World Bank (1996) and M. Schiff (1995).

15 Smith (1982), Book I, Chapter XI, Part II, p. 269.

16 NACLA (1975), p. 10, citing Hightower (1973).

17 All the data were found on the ICO's website, «www.ico.org», in the Statistics/Historical Data section. They are based on monthly average prices; at the time of writing the UK retail prices for 2006 and 2007 were not yet shown.

18 Gibbon (2007), which I have already mentioned in Chapter 1.

19 Lines (2004), pp. 36–7, Table 5.

20 Bridger (2007), p. 9.

21 Ibid., p. 7.

22 Nissanke and Thorbecke (2007), pp. 24 and 230.

23 Graffham (2007), p. 1.

24 Data from the FAO's website at «faostat.fao.org/site/336/Desktop Default.aspx?PageID=336» (October 2007).

25 Paper in Science by Justin Brashares and Andrew Balmford, reported in National Geographic News on 11 November 2004. May be downloaded at «www.seaaroundus.org/OtherWebsites/2004/AfricanBushMeattrade.pdf» (January 2008).

26 Gupta (2004).

27 Daviron and Ponte (2005), p. 86.

28 The breakdown of the former aluminium system is analysed in Lines (1989, 1990).

29 Banana Link (2005), p. 2.

30 Business Times (2005).

31 The Telegraph (2006).

32 WTO (2006).

33 Traidcraft (2005), p. 3.

34 See Oxfam International (2002), pp. 20–7.

35 UNCTAD (2003a) Table A.2.

4
Not farming but gambling

Who rolls the dice?

The charity Oxfam quoted this remark about business arrangements by an apple farmer in South Africa:

> I talked to my financial manager the other day … and he said, 'When you deliver your fruit, who do you invoice?' I said no one and that I wait for the price to be told to me. He said, 'You're not farming, you're gambling.'[1]

As we have seen, farming for a living is something of a gamble at the best of times, bearing in mind the vagaries of the weather, pests, diseases and prices. Yet under this arrangement, the farmer does not know the price of the produce even when it has been sold. This has become quite a common experience around the world. The farmer might not even be sure whether the presumed buyer will take it, since there is frequently no written contract even if they trade with each other regularly. If the purchasing company is oversupplied or not fully satisfied with the produce, it can simply refuse to take delivery. That can happen even when the farmer is exporting to the other side of the world. These arrangements leave all the risk on the farmer's side, even though in most cases the company will be much better equipped to handle it.

Large companies operate in all areas of agricultural trade, and at every stage of the supply chain:
- in agricultural production itself, owning and running their own farms or plantations;
- in national and international trade (Cargill and Bunge in the grain trade, for example, or Volcafé and Neumann in coffee);

- in processing agricultural produce into goods for sale (as in roasting coffee beans, making chocolate, refining sugar or preparing ready-made meals for supermarkets to sell);
- and in wholesaling and retailing.

The same company can operate at several of these stages at once. For example, the firms that supply rich countries with tropical fruit, such as bananas and pineapples, usually own plantations and shipping lines as well as trading the fruit and supplying wholesalers and retailers. Most farmers also have to rely on small numbers of corporate suppliers for their inputs such as seeds and fertilizers, as well as such buyers' markets for their sales. They are therefore vulnerable to price and other pressures on both sides of their business and can easily find they are squeezed between them. But the shape has been changing in recent years as supermarkets have come to dominate food retailing. The supermarkets have acquired great power over the chain, while earlier stages have become less profitable for farmers and corporations alike. This has led to the decline and in some places the complete loss of other marketing channels for farmers' produce. However, in some markets agro-processing firms (such as coffee roasters), integrated production and trading companies (as in the banana sector) and trading companies (especially in bulk crops like cereals and soya beans) remain important. As a paper by UNCTAD put it,

> The growing literature on commodity prices and commodity-dependent countries reveals a 'disconnect' between prices paid by final consumers and those received by producers, because of higher profits at later stages of the value chain. The stage in the value chain where concentration is largest tends to acquire a large share of the profits, with a smaller share of the final price going to the other stages.... While African producers have incurred income losses, traders and firms in the higher steps of the value chain have been reaping significant benefits.[2]

This chapter will examine these trends, discuss their implications for agriculture in poor countries and consider what can be done about them. As hinted by UNCTAD (although not explicitly stated), the basic issue is one of power over the supply chain.

Agricultural production has always been fragmented among thousands or indeed millions of farmers with small plots of land. In the past, food processing and retailing were almost as fragmented too; indeed, much of the world's food processing is still done in the farm's own household, for example when pounding corn to prepare it for the family's meal. On the other hand, a generation or two ago the governments of developing countries themselves played an influential role in international agricultural trade. Following the example set by many developed countries (including the UK in its domestic agriculture), they assisted their farmers through national marketing boards which bought the export crops and sold them on the world's markets. Among other benefits, this gave exporting countries considerable bargaining power, which their farmers lack without marketing boards to intermediate on their behalf. In many cases, the boards were abolished under structural adjustment and private traders took their place.

At the other end of the chain, ownership in food retailing has become more concentrated and the chains have become 'buyer-led'. As most developed countries' retailing markets approach saturation point, supermarket chains have expanded with extraordinary rapidity across the rest of the world, with their share of retail food sales in both South America and East Asia 'ballooning' from less than 20 per cent to more than 50 per cent between 1992 and 2002, according to the FAO.[3] In most of the world this trend has been led by supermarkets from developed countries, especially Europe and the US, but in Africa by investment from South Africa.[4] An interesting contrast exists between China, where supermarkets reached 48 per cent of urban food retailing in 2001, largely as a result of foreign investment,[5] and India, where their share of food retailing was estimated at only 5 per cent in 2003[6] and foreign investment in retailing is prohibited. Even the US giant Wal-Mart could invest only in a wholesale joint venture with an Indian firm, Bharti Enterprises.[7] Domestic Indian supermarket firms are expanding, but they meet resistance which has sometimes forced newly opened stores to close.[8]

Central planning

This is not the first time that agriculture has been in such a predicament. Consider these words written in 1939 by a former British Minister of Agriculture:

> It cannot be contended nowadays that it is impossible to manage prices so as to introduce stability into them. The real questions are: Who is to do the managing? And for what purpose? Is it to be done by powerful corporations for the purpose of making as much profit as possible, or is it to be done on behalf of the community with the general well-being as the end in view? The pace towards the former method has been very rapid during the past twenty years, and the longer society shirks its duty in undertaking its responsibilities, the more difficult they will become. Free competition never was a safeguard for the people.[9]

The same argument can be heard almost word for word today. The supply management proposals of Chapter 3 cannot succeed without tackling the problem of corporate buyer power. As we saw there, the exact balance of power varies from market to market, but whichever element is dominant exerts its control of the chain through the detailed management of its own supplies, in the system of supply chain management. This was rendered easier with the development of information technology in the 1980s and 1990s. In a supermarket company, sales of each product in every store are closely monitored, and a central control system ensures that exactly the right amounts are delivered every day to meet expected demand. These methods, coupled with transportation by airfreight, enable precision of supply even when importing perishable seasonal goods like fruit and vegetables from other continents.

In general, there has also been an increase in the indirect control of production and initial processing by the TNCs, for example via outgrower schemes, in which small farms grow produce to order. This further reinforces the buyer-driven character of the supply chains. There is little sign that companies at the buyer end now want to start running production operations themselves; because of the weak contractual position described above, the buyers are happy to source produce from others since the methods of supply chain management give them effective control over the process anyway. The purchasing firm thereby keeps its overheads down, it is relieved of direct responsibility for employment and does not have to bear the losses if demand falls short or the produce is not desired for other reasons. In all these respects, the situation is similar to the outsourced production of clothes, shoes and other industrial products, or call centres and financial back offices in service sectors of the economy. In the US, it was described thus in an eloquent magazine article which we will return to below: 'The problem is that Wal-Mart ... does not participate in the market so much as use its power to micromanage the market, carefully coordinating the actions of thousands of firms from a position above the market.'[10] Had the term not acquired another meaning elsewhere, supply chain management might well be called 'central planning'.

Nevertheless, in their home markets most supermarkets compete fiercely among themselves and derive low financial margins from their selling operations in the stores. The four companies that dominate UK food retailing are reported to have average profit margins of 4.5 per cent of sales, compared with 8.5 per cent at leading processing firms such as Procter & Gamble and Cadbury Schweppes.[11] In practice the supermarkets continue to work to an old dictum of the 1960s and 1970s: 'Pile 'em high and sell 'em cheap.' Their immense bargaining power enables them to continually press their suppliers for more advantageous terms, which they can achieve due to the size of throughput, and increasingly also as a result of the lack of alternative outlets. Although their profits may not be high as a percentage of turnover, they provide good returns on capital due to the large economies of scale that the firms can exploit.

However, in some markets the processing stage is still the locus of market power. Some food processing companies have been able to stay in the game with the ownership of a strong brand. In the case of coffee, a wave of mergers in the 1990s concentrated the market in a handful of global firms, which now control leading national brands such as Jacobs and Douwe-Egberts as well as long-established global ones like Nescafé. It was recently estimated that the two largest companies controlled 57 per cent of the world market for roasted and instant coffees, and the top five some 87 per cent. Market concentration in international coffee trading is almost as high, with the top three companies estimated to handle around 45 per cent.[12] To get the measure of this, it means that each of the two largest roaster companies (Nestlé and Kraft Foods, which happen to be two of the three largest agrifood companies of all) purchases well over 30 million standard 60kg bags of coffee every year, and the three largest trading firms buy and sell about 18 million bags each, while the world's 25 million or so coffee farmers produce on average about five bags each. That is a measure of the imbalance of bargaining power along the supply chain.

Control of the coffee market has been managed since the late 1990s by a system known as supplier-managed inventory, according to which the *suppliers* are responsible for maintaining the stocks used by the purchasing firm, even if the stocks are held at a port in that firm's country or even in its own factory. This reduces the working capital required by the roaster company for maintaining stocks, and enables it to ensure its purchases exactly match daily or weekly demand: the same as is achieved by the supermarkets through outsourcing and other means. In this way, any oversupply on the market is held either by the roaster's immediate suppliers or still further back along the supply chain. The price of the roasters' raw material is thereby kept down, while the high degree of market concentration at their stage of the supply chain, reinforced by their strong brand names, ensures that their own selling prices can stay up. They can therefore steadily increase the margins and profits they acquire from the business.

The 25 largest food and agribusiness companies (excluding retailers) are reported to come from just eight countries. Only one of them is even partially owned outside the developed world: the brewing company Interbrew AmBev, which is jointly owned in Belgium and Brazil and was listed in 2004 as the sixteenth-largest agro-food firm with annual sales of US$10.7 billion.[13] However, some of the highest margins in consumer trade are found among export commodities in which developing countries specialize. The supermarkets' margins vary considerably according to product group, but for fruit and vegetables they can be as high as 30 or even 40 per cent in the UK.[14] Coffee margins for the roaster corporations are another notable example. In the early 1980s their gross margins were fairly stable at around 80 US cents per pound weight, but 20 years later they had risen to a plateau of about $1.80 per pound; meanwhile, coffee import prices fell from about $1.60 per pound in 1980 to little over 50 cents per pound in 2002.[15] Oxfam quoted an analyst's report which said that nothing else in food and beverages was 'remotely as good' as Nestlé's market share, size of sales and profit margins on coffee. Nestlé was estimated to make between 26 and 30 pence of profit for every pound's worth of instant coffee sold.[16]

Many companies further back on the supply chains find that they are losing a dominant position to the supermarkets. Those that have lost out the most appear to be vertically integrated firms that traditionally controlled a chain directly, owning their own plantations, trading and processing operations, but no retail outlets. They emerged in an earlier era, when producers were more powerful and there was not the same concentration in retailing as today. In the banana trade three integrated TNCs controlled 47 per cent of the world market as long ago as 1966,[17] but even the banana corporations (led by the US firms Dole, Del Monte and Chiquita) are losing control as the supermarkets have become 'price makers', obliging the TNCs to accept the prices they offer. Thus when, in 2003, ASDA in the UK cut its margin on bananas from 32 per cent to 22 per cent to gain a competitive advantage with a lower shop price, its competitors met the challenge by reducing the prices they paid their suppliers, rather than their own margins.[18] Four years later ASDA (a subsidiary of Wal-Mart) again cut its prices by 20 per cent, and its competitors followed suit within hours.[19] As a result of this sort of price pressure, plantation workers' daily wages in Costa Rica fell from around US$12–15 per day in 2000 to $7–8 in 2003.[20]

And similar pressures have even damaged as mighty a

corporation as Kraft, however well defended it may be on the coffee market: 'Since 2004, Kraft has announced plans to ... eliminate a quarter of its products.... Even as costs rise ... discounters continue to demand that Kraft lower its prices further. Kraft has found itself with no other choice than to swallow the costs, and hence to tear itself to pieces.'[21]

And small farmers?

Power over agricultural supply chains enables the big firms to pick and choose who will supply them. However, even though their bigger size is such an advantage to them, in most cases they would rather purchase from small numbers of large farms and other suppliers than from large numbers of small farms. This may seem paradoxical. However, such trade is easier to organize, and larger farms and plantations can be run in a more businesslike manner, themselves benefiting from economies of scale. The purchasers therefore tend to prefer few, highly capitalized suppliers which themselves use intensive, tightly controlled production methods. In any case, the prices of many products fell too low to permit any producer that lacks economies of scale to prosper. An instructive case is found in Kenya, the country which in the late 1950s pioneered the outsourcing of agricultural production under contract as a way of getting *smallholdings* to grow tea for export rather than plantations or 'tea estates', as was the norm elsewhere. Things have changed there now, at least in the country's successful horticultural sector. A clue to this puzzle is found at the end of this quotation:

> Smallholders traditionally were the backbone of the Kenya export horticulture trade, comprising 70 per cent of production, marketing individually or as groups. But by the late 1990s, 40 per cent of the products for export came from the farms or leased land of exporters such as Homegrown Ltd, 42 per cent from large commercial farms, and only 18 per cent from smallholders.... Dolan and Humphrey found that the top seven exporters controlled over 75 per cent of all exports by the end of the 1990s.... This shakeout ... is due in large measure to supermarkets'

preference for sourcing from large firms 'capable of assuming responsibility for the rigid enforcement of standards'.[22]

As we shall see later in this chapter, the importance of supplying produce that meets the purchasing companies' exacting requirements has become critical. This is especially true with the supermarkets; but it tends to marginalize smaller farms and reinforces the crisis they face. In Latin America the consequences have been spelt out in these words: 'Supermarkets, who operate on a contract basis, prefer to work with large farm operators. . . . This increase in competition has gradually squeezed out small farmers. . . . In subsector after subsector, small farmers are being excluded from the *domestic* value chain.'[23] Elsewhere, according to the FAO, 'In less than five years, Thailand's leading supermarket chain pared its list of vegetable suppliers from 250 down to just 10.' And in Brazil, more than 75,000 dairy farmers were 'delisted' by the 12 largest milk processers between 1997 and 2001.[24] This trend puts further pressure on smaller, poorer and more remote farms and countries and leads to growing landlessness, rural poverty and dependency.

This trend is appearing everywhere. In the UK it was reported:

Kevin Hawkins, the director-general of the British Retail Consortium, the retailers' trade body ... says that it is 'no accident' that small fruit and vegetable growers generate more hard-luck stories than other suppliers. Sour grapes are alleged.

'That sector is heavily populated by small businesses and over the past few years all retailers have been consolidating their supplier bases – giving more volume to fewer suppliers – in order to achieve economies of scale. Some of these suppliers have, as a result, been delisted, he argues.[25]

Meanwhile, in China a US government report gave this advice in favour of consolidating farms into larger units within vertically integrated, buyer-led supply chains:

The maturing of the retail sector in China is also beginning to affect the way food is produced at the farm level.... To keep pace with the demand of buyers, *farms will have to adjust* by specializing in a particular commodity, consolidating fragmented land holdings to achieve scale economies, and forging stronger links with processors and retailers. Closer relationships between firms at different stages of production and marketing are emerging as larger commercialized farm operations grow produce and animals under contract for processors, retailers or exporters. This trend is likely to continue and may profoundly alter the way food is produced in China.[26]

Another clue is found in this comment by a leading academic critic: 'Large retailers and brand-name companies are particularly vulnerable to consumer campaigns. The easiest way to contain risks of this sort is to work with fewer and larger suppliers.'[27] In the largest supermarket firms, central control of *global* supplies seems already to be on its way: Carrefour, France's largest chain, switched to buying melons from just three growers in north-east Brazil to supply all its Brazilian stores and ship to distribution centres in as many as 21 countries.[28]

As we saw in Chapter 2, leading purchasers are concentrating their purchases as between exporting countries, with the coffee roasting companies showing a marked preference to buy from the three biggest-cropping countries, Brazil, Vietnam and Colombia. This is partly a consequence of supplier-managed inventory. Countries with smaller crops can lose out even if the high quality of their product is renowned, as in the cases of Guatemala, Kenya and Ethiopia for coffee. But the biggest losers once again are the very smallest and poorest countries, many of them in Africa.

This poses a colossal dilemma for rural development. Is there any long-term future on present trends for smallholders and subsistence or semi-subsistence farmers in poor countries? If not, what can be done about it? Should large farms and plantations be encouraged as the best source of future rural production and employment? What then will happen to all the people who currently depend on smallholdings? And what about the environmental consequences, which are already severe, with the implications for soil quality, water resources and deforestation of the transfer to large-scale, intensive agriculture? Well-known examples include the threat to orang-utans in Indonesia because of deforestation to establish oil palm plantations; the severe impact of monoculture production and extremely high use of pesticides in banana plantations, many of which are set up where rainforest has been cleared; and the monoculture cropping of soya in Brazil, Argentina and Paraguay.

Abusive relationships

As a result of the supermarkets' ability to thrive with low resale margins, competition from them can be devastating not just for small farms but for smaller shops; at the same time, the higher margins they can attain on fresh fruit and vegetables make that sector particularly attractive for them to expand into. However, it is the low margins available to them on a broad range of sales that explain why they press *all* their suppliers so relentlessly, in a constant effort to reduce costs. A small reduction in purchase prices can significantly improve their margins and final profits, giving a supermarket a competitive advantage over its rivals. The advantages that accrue from company size were illustrated in an official finding in the UK:

> The bigger a retailer is, the better able it is to extract lower prices from suppliers. This was a finding from the UK Competition Commission's investigation into the UK supermarket sector in 2000.... The biggest supermarket – in this case Tesco – consistently paid suppliers 4 per cent below the industry average, while smaller supermarkets paid above the average rate.[29]

So naturally, Tesco could win higher margins yielding bigger profits, and so invest more to increase its market dominance still further.

In the effort to increase financial returns, supermarkets have devised numerous 'out-of-store' methods to reduce costs and even extract payments from their suppliers, in addition to the regular in-store mark-up on the purchase price. Some of these practices can seem underhand to anyone used to areas of business in which purchasers do not enjoy such market power. Most of these practices pass business risk back from the retailer to its immediate suppliers and through them to the primary producers. Super-markets have been known to extract allowances or payments from their suppliers by such techniques as:

- Rebates and discounts, which can be declared unilaterally *after* deliveries are made. For example, a British fruit supplier was quoted as receiving £1.40 out of a leading supermarket's retail price of £1.90 per punnet of strawberries. Out of this he paid a regular fee of 5 per cent to a middleman, but it was often supplemented by a 'rebate' of up to 7 per cent, which represented the middleman's compulsory 'contribution' to the supermarket's marketing costs.
- Charging suppliers for all ancillary costs, including the transport of produce to the supermarket's warehouse, packaging (from a manufacturer nominated by the supermarket), labelling, and even rent for plastic trays on which the produce is displayed in the shops.
- Late payment of invoices, for example 60 days after delivery – terms that few but the biggest farming businesses in poor countries are in any position to accept.
- Promotional expenses, for example when the retail price of an item is lowered for a short period or extra produce is given away, and the resultant discount is deducted from the price paid to the supplier rather than the supermarket's margin. We saw earlier how this happened with banana sales. In this way it is farmers and plantation workers who actually pay for 'buy-one-get-one-free' and other cheap offers.
- Charging a branded supplier for shelf space assigned to its products, or other suppliers for shelf space used during price promotions. There can also be upfront charges for listing new products in a company's stores. Leading British supermarkets can reportedly require payments of £300,000 (US$600,000) in return for shelf space for a new product; their manner in doing so has been said to be 'often demanding and aggressive'.[30]

In the US, it has been argued that Wal-Mart's aim is 'to remake entirely how its suppliers do business, not least so that it can shift many of its own costs of doing business onto them. Wal-Mart ... dictates how they package their products, how they ship those products, and how they gather and process information on the movement of those products.'[31]

Oxfam described the loose contractual arrangements that are found in many areas of export horticulture (as well as in many supermarkets' purchases from farms in their own country); it is these practices that enable the special price and payment terms to be demanded:

> Agreements are often verbal, so there is no written contract to break.... Such informality gives buyers flexibility to delay payments, break programmes, or cancel orders, forcing suppliers to find last-minute alternatives. 'They chop and change their minds constantly,' according to an apple packhouse manager in South Africa. 'It takes one month for us to get the fruit there, but it takes two minutes for them to change their minds ... then the only thing we can do is dump it somewhere else.'... Supermarkets fix the margins they want and leave suppliers and farmers to bear any price fluctuations.[32]

Oxfam explained the human implications in this way: 'Delivery schedules for fresh produce are extremely tight. Cut flowers and baby vegetables are airfreighted from Kenya and Zambia to the UK, with supermarkets placing their orders for produce to be sent the same day. For ... women workers, same-day orders mean long and unforeseen overtime.'[33]

A leading British supermarket director was reported as objecting that, 'You can't commit to 20,000 punnets of strawberries three months in advance. You just wouldn't.'[34] But every farmer has to commit to the amounts they sow much more than three months before the harvest; and they do not have the financial strength available to the supermarkets to withstand the market fluctuations that follow. These constraints are felt not only by suppliers in South Africa or Kenya, but even by large companies in the US:

> Today's dominant firms ... are programmed to cut cost faster than price.... The effects ... are clear: We see them in the collapsing profit margins of the firms caught in Wal-Mart's system. We see them in the fact that of Wal-Mart's top ten suppliers in 1994, four have sought bankruptcy protection.[35]

The supermarkets' market power enables them to acquire fresh produce from around the world throughout the year, overcoming the constraints of the seasons, and to extend their range into ever more exotic items produced in other climate zones. Their push for fresh produce explains much of the pressure on developing countries to export horticultural products such as fruit, vegetables and cut flowers, under the banner of diversifying into non-traditional commodities. When the prices of *traditional* commodities such as coffee and cotton have been so badly squeezed, the arguments in favour are appealing. However, as we see, the supply chains are every bit as tightly controlled as on the traditional markets, and the constraints of delivering on them are as narrow. And we have also seen that, Kenya excepted, this has produced little or no economic benefit for poor countries in Africa.

More hoops to jump through

If a farmer receives a bad price for some produce, or has to make special payments to the purchaser in order to maintain sales, that produce is nevertheless sold. However, the ability to achieve such sales on the rich world's markets is being made progressively more difficult as ever stricter standards are imposed on the health, safety, size, appearance, pesticide residues and other attributes of products on sale. Consumers in Western Europe and North America have become concerned about food safety, environmental costs (seen in the growing demand for organic produce and complaints about the 'food miles' that produce traverses before it reaches the supermarket) and genetic modification. Possessing vast spending power as they do, they can find it hard to understand any reason why their high standards should not be met. Supermarkets respond by imposing their own strict and detailed requirements on their suppliers.

The ostensible purpose of the WTO and its predecessor, the GATT, is to widen international access to member countries' markets, by limiting import tariffs and other statutory obstacles. But formal access of this sort does not guarantee an ability to actually *enter* a market and trade in it.[36] Within the EU, all food products sold must comply with the same legal requirements, no matter where in the world they were produced. The hygienic or technical standards required can themselves act as serious barriers to the chances of a farmer's produce reaching the rich world's shops. An UNCTAD report objected that such standards provide an 'implicit incentive to create an institutional structure of food controls that is equivalent to the one in importing countries';[37] in view of the huge worldwide disparities in levels of income, technology and infrastructure that we have observed, this seems a quite unrealistic requirement to impose.

These impediments to market entry can be authorized under governmental rules and intergovernmental frameworks, or by purchasing firms themselves. For both public and private standards, the need for some coordination became apparent, so that produce that met the requirements of one importing country or purchasing firm would also be acceptable to another. Two founding agreements of the WTO in 1995 were drawn up to meet this need in the case of public standards.[38] In principle, private standards set by commercial firms are meant to come under them too. However, the system has operated far from perfectly, partly because, as in the WTO more widely, developing countries have not had much influence over the decisions reached. Changes to national standards have to be officially notified to the WTO, but they often depart from agreed norms, while in many cases insufficient time has been allowed to exporting countries to adapt to the changes required.[39] Problems have also arisen when, for example, pesticides have been banned and appropriate replacements were not available in developing countries, and when maximum permitted pesticide residues in a food product have been reduced and it has been difficult for poor countries to meet the new levels reliably.[40]

But modern commercial standards tend to be even stricter than those laid down by law. They can be especially troublesome for smallholder farms, which do not have the facilities or the detailed records that large farms and plantations maintain. For example, a recent proposal to require suppliers to keep detailed worker records, including copies of contracts and payslips, is quite impractical in rural parts of many of the poorest countries, except for the largest farm employers.[41] In 1997 a group of leading

European supermarket firms formed a set of common standards known as EurepGAP. Its potential power is seen in the fact that between them, 30 members of the working group control 85 per cent of fresh produce sales in the EU.[42] Since all of their suppliers everywhere have to meet these requirements, they soon became akin to a worldwide set of commercial standards. A revised version was introduced in 2000 and another in 2007 – when, revealingly, the title was changed to GlobalGAP.[43]

The development of universal private standards has been controversial from the beginning. For most farmers in poor countries it is expensive. A study of a group of farmers in Zambia found that their farming and managerial skills improved when meeting the requirements of EurepGAP, but at a cost per individual grower of £4,664 for initial investments and £938 annually to maintain the system. The authors concluded: 'Given the farmers' levels of income from export sales these figures are obviously untenable. Massive levels of donor support [from foreign aid agencies] made it possible to achieve EurepGAP but as donor support only has a limited life it would not be possible to maintain EurepGAP certification unaided.'[44] It has been objected that, 'The initial EurepGAP protocol … was imposed on developing-country suppliers without any prior consultation or impact assessment';[45] while after the second version was introduced:

> Representatives of 'developing' country producers have expressed alarm at the 'imposition' of EUREP-GAP standards by retailers without due consideration of local conditions. They claim that current standards (1) favour large-scale producers and threaten the livelihoods of 'hundreds of thousands of people' in exporting countries such as Kenya, and (2) become in effect a barrier to market entry.[46]

These systems of external control over supplies are closely linked with the business practices described in the previous section, and with consumer pressures in the rich countries. Private standards can also be used to extract money from suppliers, as illustrated by a British fruit supplier who said that, 'For every damaged or mouldy strawberry that a customer complains about, the supermarket slaps a flat-rate fine of £10 on the supplier.'[47] As income gaps between countries have widened, these problems of market entry have grown worse, since consumers' expectations in the rich countries are running far ahead of the poorest countries' ability to meet them. On the positive side, one of the consumers' concerns is for the welfare of people who produce their food and the impact of production processes on their environments. This can lead to campaigns for farmers to get higher and more secure prices (mostly via fairtrade), and against child labour and other employment abuses; and to opposition to genetically modified crops and a growing demand for organic produce. But even in these areas, suppliers have to be certified as reaching a certain standard, often at a cost to themselves of several hundred pounds; and there is concern about the proliferation of private certification standards involved. However, at least in the case of fairtrade the farmers are assured of higher prices and payment in advance, plus a further share of the earnings which they can use to improve their communities in other ways.

Much of the discussion on this topic has been about standards for horticulture, especially fruit and vegetables, but GlobalGAP's ambitions are seen in the breadth of its new integrated set of standards – as well as in what they omit. According to its own publicity, the applications range all the way from 'plant and livestock production to plant propagation materials and compound feed manufacturing'; they cover seven crop categories (from fruit and vegetables to cotton), five categories of livestock and five of aquaculture.[48] The standards were 'primarily designed to reassure consumers about how food is produced on the farm by minimising detrimental environmental impacts of farming operations, reducing the use of chemical inputs and ensuring a responsible approach to worker health and safety as well as animal welfare.'[49] So animal welfare is assured – but not the living wages of agricultural workers or adequate prices for the farmers.

As a consequence of the pressures and power plays that pass along the supply chains, the longest-established of all international standards are themselves frequently ignored. These are the employment norms embodied in the conventions of the International Labour Organization (ILO), which have the status of international treaties and are therefore binding both under international law and in the domestic law of all countries that ratify them. However, as has been reported:

> In many countries that export [fresh fruit and vegetables], like the Philippines, Thailand, Kenya and Indonesia, the right to freely organise is acknowledged by law. In practise however workers find it difficult to join free trade unions and to carry out union activities like collective bargaining or exercising their right to strike. Costa Rican legislation, for instance, acknowledges freedom of association but in practice agricultural workers do not have the freedom to associate and/or to form a trade union. Brazilian legislation also acknowledges the right to freedom of association, but particularly in rural areas, workers who actually make use of this freedom encounter serious resistance from employers.[50]

The requirements of international purchasers, it seems, have greater weight than either international or domestic laws. Whose standards are really being maintained: those of the rich world's pampered consumers or of the poor world, whose labour is used to serve them?

Is breaking up so hard to do?

The dangers of power within a market being concentrated in the hands of one participant, or a few of them, have been known since the birth of capitalism. They were described thus in 1776 by Adam Smith, the father of modern economics: 'The monopolists, by keeping the market constantly understocked, by never fully supplying the effectual demand, sell their commodities much above the natural price, and raise their emoluments [earnings] ... greatly above the natural rate.'[51] This describes, almost by name, an exploitative form of corporate supply management. Smith also observed a general tendency among what he called 'the dealers' (those who lived by profit on 'stock' – what we now call capitalists):

To widen the market and to narrow the competition is always the interest of the dealers. To widen the market may frequently be agreeable enough to the interest of the public; but to narrow the competition must always be against it, and can serve only to enable the dealers, by raising their profits above what they naturally would be, to levy, for their own benefit, an absurd tax upon the rest of their fellow-citizens.[52]

In 1890, exactly one hundred years after Smith died, the US passed the first legislation to counter concentrations of ownership in business: what in US parlance is called anti-trust policy and elsewhere is described as competition policy. The Sherman Act (named after its author, a Republican senator) was intended to prevent collaborative arrangements that would increase the cost of goods to the customer.[53] The act was famously used in 1911 to break up the Standard Oil company; in the same year there was also an attempt to break up US Steel, the dominant steel company of the time, but it was unsuccessful. In recent memory, the US government acted to break up the AT&T telephone monopoly in 1984, and more recently threatened Microsoft with break-up for alleged monopoly in computer operating systems. So in the world's most successful and productive economy there is a history of using competition laws against some of the most powerful corporations, even at the risk of losing efficiencies they derive from economies of scale. It has been argued that the 1911 Standard Oil decision 'was based flatly on the assumption that the need to ensure robust competition sometimes outweighs the benefits of near-term efficiency. Standard's roll-up of the oil industry [had] cut the cost of kerosene by nearly 70 per cent, and yet the justices shattered the firm into thirty-four pieces.'[54]

The Sherman Act has been emulated in many other countries, including the UK, where the Monopolies Commission was founded in 1948. In the EU, a whole section of the European Commission is devoted to enforcing competition. The basis everywhere has lain in the notion that anti-competitive practices are found among the producers of goods or services, who use monopolistic pricing to take advantage of their customers. The Standard Oil and US Steel cases were both conducted against companies that sold primary commodities – a basic fuel and a basic industrial metal, respectively. The situation we witness, however, has turned this on its head. Buyer power on modern supply chains raises corporations' 'emoluments' (in Adam Smith's word) not by understocking a market and failing to satisfy effectual demand, but by using various tricks so as not to absorb available supply, thereby keeping the producer end of the supply chain *over*stocked.

Present-day laws are ill-adapted to this situation. Competition policy, as defined in the leading industrial countries, has not caught up with it. It was designed to deal with cases of monopoly and oligopoly, but in modern agricultural markets fragmentary producers are squeezed by market concentration at the buyer's end of the chain. The words 'monopoly' and 'oligopoly' do not even fit here, since they refer to market power on the supply side. In these supply chains, power resides on the buyer's, or demand, side – among supermarkets, coffee-roasting companies and so on. The right word happens to be one of the ugliest in the vocabulary of economics: oligopsony. Politically it is also harder to deal with: consumers (who are also the voters in a democracy) will rarely find much sympathy with monopoly prices, but they may be less concerned if far-away rural people's incomes are squeezed to ensure that prices in their own shops remain low.

What then can be done? At times, the developed countries' governments have appeared to egg on the process of buyer power, or, at best, accept it as a fact of life without thinking about its implications. The British High Commission is reported to have assisted Tesco's lobbying of the New Delhi government for entry into Indian retailing, no doubt simply on the grounds of supporting a big British company. But there has slowly developed a softly spoken, but quite widespread, understanding among many observers that, besides supply management, some substantial strengthening and reforms of competition policy are required to deal with this problem, including their application at the global level (and not just nationally or regionally as at present). That seems only fitting in a world where markets have become global, as we are constantly told. If concern for poverty is to be anything more than just words, this must surely be placed high on the international agenda.

However, the task is not easy and there are many different ideas on how to do it. Global measures need to be introduced to address corporate concentration not just among supermarkets but in the areas of processing and trade, as well as farmers' supplies such as seeds, fertilizers and fuel. They should apply not just to single firms but to small groups of companies that dominate a market. This is especially important in connection with supermarkets, which are acquiring great international power but in the developed world remain highly concentrated at the national level only. There have been repeated calls for at least some official monitoring of corporate concentrations in international food supply chains. With a few exceptions (such as Wal-Mart's ownership of ASDA in the UK and Aldi's expansion into Germany's neighbouring countries), the supermarkets have been extending their interests mainly into poorer countries rather than into each other's markets among the rich countries. The UN used to do such monitoring until its Centre for Transnational Corporations was closed down in 1992.[55] Others have called for a WTO rule that would require member states to provide information on state trading enterprises' activities to be extended to private-sector companies too. A database could be compiled, which should be accessible to the public online.[56]

As part of its mandate, a global competition authority should strictly regulate the purchasing practices of global corporations. National and regional authorities (including the EU) should do likewise, extending the scope of their competition policies to cover buying practices and concentrations among a few companies on the purchasing side.[57] Policies were developed in the US in the 1930s and 1950s to counter predatory business practices, and these should be revived in other countries. Some countries, such as France, have gone some way down this path,[58] but this approach needs to be generalized. The problem would then be tackled from both ends: by attacking with competition policy corporate concentration itself, which gives these companies their power; and by picking off the methods they use to exploit that power. However, in France these measures are actually under threat from President Nicolas Sarkozy's new, economically liberal government, with proposals to end a ban on shops selling goods for less than they paid for them, and the easing of restrictions on passing the costs of promotional offers back to suppliers. It was reported that a federation of leading agri-processing corporations (including Danone and Procter & Gamble) objected to such an 'ultraliberal system' coming in.[59]

In line with the century-old US precedent of the Sherman Act, the rules should also include the mandatory break-up of companies with excessive market shares, whether on the selling or the buying side of the business. There should be much stronger controls to prevent such concentrations from developing in the first place, and others to break up companies if they have developed. This would increase farmers' relative negotiating strength, raise farmgate prices and at last return some say to farmers over how the supply chains operate. The best institutional base for this is not yet clear and it would be premature to make any precise recommendations at this stage. What matters is to press for the principle to be accepted in international quarters, and for action then to be taken on it. Intriguingly, something like it seems to be accepted by the head of Wal-Mart himself: 'Last year, Wal-Mart [Chief Executive Officer] Lee Scott called on the British government to take antitrust action against the UK grocery chain Tesco. Whenever a firm nears a 30 per cent share of any market, Scott said, "there is a point where government is compelled to intervene."'[60]

We already know that this can be done since it has been done before, against a precursor of Wal-Mart as the dominant super-market chain in the US. This was the Great Atlantic & Pacific Tea Company (better known as the A&P), whose story was told in the article in *Harper's* magazine which have just quoted.[61] The US federal government took repeated actions against this firm between 1915 and 1949, when the Justice Department finally sued for it to be dismembered under the Sherman Act. The story is much less well-known than that of Standard Oil but not, as one might think, because the attempt to break up the A&P eventually failed while the

Standard Oil case succeeded. On the contrary, in the long run this series of actions proved *more* successful in debilitating the grocery firm, as a result of which both it and the story are largely forgotten now. Standard Oil survives in several giant oil companies which it spawned, including both halves of ExxonMobil, the biggest of them all. But although the A&P remained intact, it shrank in size in the 1960s and 1970s, and in 1979 its remnants were acquired by a German firm.[62] In 2007 it had no more than 337 stores,[63] compared with 15,737 in 1930.[64] Determined public action against dominant corporate power evidently can work, without apparently causing any serious economic harm to set against the huge benefits it can deliver.

Notes

1   Oxfam International (2004), p. 70.
2   UNCTAD (2003b), p. 24.
3   FAO (2004b), p. 20.
4   Reardon *et al.* (2003b), p. 6.
5   Reardon *et al.* (2003a), p. 4.
6   Reardon *et al.* (2003b), p. 7.
7   Reuters (2007).
8   Buncombe (2007).
9   Addison (1939), pp. 122–3.
10 Lynn (2006), p. 2 of 10. (The page number refers to a computer print-out of Lynn's article downloaded from the Internet, not the original page number in *Harper's* magazine.)
11 Hall (2007).
12 Agritrade (2007).
13 Rabobank International (2004), p. 16.
14 Oxfam International (2004), p. 68.
15 Daviron and Ponte (2005), p. 206.
16 Oxfam International (2002), p. 26, citing Deutsche Bank, 'Soluble Coffee: a Pot of Gold?' (2000).
17 UNCTAD and Common Fund (2004), p. 5.
18 van de Kasteele and van der Stichele (2005), p. 29.
19 Banana Link (2007), p. 1.
20 Brown and Sander (2007), p. 10, citing Vorley and Fox (2004b), p. 22.
21 Lynn (2006), p. 2 of 10.

22 Vorley (2003), p. 69, citing S. Friedberg, 'The Contradictions of Clean: Supermarket ethical trade and African horticulture', in *Gatekeeper* 109 (London: IIED, 2003) (emphasis added by Vorley).

23 Imber *et al.* (2003), p. 31 (emphasis added), citing T. Reardon, E. Farina & J. Berdegue, 'Globalization, Changing Market Institutions and Agrifood Systems in Latin America: Implications for the poor's livelihoods', in 74th EAAE Seminar, Livelihoods and Rural Poverty: Technology, policy and institutions, 12–15 September 2001, Imperial College at Wye, UK.

24 FAO (2004b), p. 21.

25 Hall (2007), p. 2 in the Internet version.

26 Gale (2002), p. 16 (emphasis added).

27 Humphrey (2000), p. 2.

28 FAO (2004b), p. 21.

29 ActionAid International (2005), p. 21.

30 Hall (2007). These examples also draw on Vorley (2003), p. 35, and Brown and Sander (2007), pp. 9–10.

31 Lynn (2006), p. 9 of 10.

32 Oxfam International (2004), pp. 69–70.

33 *Ibid.*, p. 71.

34 Hall (2007).

35 Lynn (2006), p. 9 of 10.

36 The distinction between formal *market access* and actual *market entry* is discussed in UNCTAD (2003c).

37 UNCTAD (2007), p. 101.

38 They cover so-called sanitary and phytosanitary measures, concerning human, animal and plant health, and technical barriers to trade, for all other matters.

39 See Pay (2005), pp. 38–50.

40 Graffham (2007), p. 4, and Pay (2005), p. 50.

41 *Ibid.*, p. 6.

42 *Ibid.*

43 See «www.globalgap.org/cms/front_content.php?idart=3&idcat= 9&lang =1» (November 2007).

44 Graffham and MacGregor (2006), p. 52.

45 UNCTAD (2007), p. 97.

46 Vorley (2003), p. 71.

47 Hall (2007).

48 «www.globalgap.org/cms/front_content.php?idcat=3» (November 2007).

49 «www.globalgap.org/cms/front_content.php?idart=3&idcat=9&lang=1» (November 2007).

50 van der Stichele *et al.* (2006), p. 21.

51 Smith (1982), Book I, Chapter VII, p. 164.

52 Smith (1982), Book I, Chapter XI, p. 358. Numerous interesting quotations from Adam Smith may be found at «www.adamsmith.org/smith/quotes.htm» (August 2007).

53 As summarized at «en.wikipedia.org/wiki/Sherman_Antitrust_Act».

54 Lynn (2006), p. 4 of 10.

55 Vorley and Fox (2004a), p. 20.

56 Murphy (2006), p. 36.

57 See ActionAid International (2005), section 4.1, and Vorley (2003), p. 75.

58 See FNSEA (2007) for a summary of French government actions in this field.

59 Maussion (2007). Of the objections from the food-processing sector she wrote (with translation by this author, emphasis from the original): 'The Danones, Procter and Gambles and other industrialists are campaigning publicly through ILEC – one of their associations – to keep the Attali Commission [originator of the proposals, named after its chairman, Jacques Attali] reined in: *"We don't want an ultraliberal system where the retailers would impose everything,"* explained Olivier Desforges, chairman of ILEC.'

60 Lynn (2006), p. 10 of 10.

61 *Ibid.*, p. 7 of 10.

62 *Ibid.*

63 «www.aptea.com/company.asp» (September 2007).

64 «www.scripophily.net/greatatandpa1.html»

5
Getting out of the trap

Can you imagine a country that was unable to grow enough food to feed the people? It would be a nation that would be subject to international pressure. It would be a nation at risk. And so when we're talking about American agriculture, we're really talking about a national security issue.

President George W. Bush, July 2001[1]

Food imports

We saw in Chapter 1 that nearly half the countries in the world fail to grow enough food to feed their people, and are therefore vulnerable to the sort of international pressure that President Bush warned about in the speech quoted above. Under structural adjustment, it was considered normal for a country to import basic foods if its comparative advantage in world markets lay in some other area of agriculture such as tea, cotton or coffee. This book has described the negative consequences of those policies for export agriculture, but they can also be devastating on the import side. In recent years the poorest countries have been importing ever more food: in sub-Saharan Africa (SSA) as a whole, bananas and yams are now the only staple foods of any consequence that are exported in greater quantities than they are imported.[2]

For many years the USSR was rendered vulnerable by its need to import large quantities of basic foods every year, most of it from the United States. As long ago as 1951 collective farming was described as 'the Achilles heel of the Soviet regime';[3] and in 1963 the USSR bought 12 million tons of grain from the US for the first time and spent one-third of its gold reserves to do so. Nikita

Khruschev, the First Secretary of the Communist Party at the time, is reported to have said of this, 'Soviet power cannot tolerate any more the shame that we had to endure';[4] the following year he was forced out of office. US grain exports to the USSR really took off after 1971, when the Nixon Administration assigned a three-year credit of $750 million to the USSR for grain purchases;[5] and Soviet grain imports reached a peak of 55 million tons in 1984–5,[6] helping to create the country's terminal crisis in the year in which Mikhail Gorbachev came to office. It has been estimated that over a period of 25 years the USSR transferred about 9,000 tonnes of gold to Western banks to purchase grain, meat, butter and other agricultural products. 'Moscow was in effect financing the development of agriculture in other countries, instead of its own,' in the words of a Russian commentator.[7] Between the 1960s and the 1980s the United States was thus able to use the 'food weapon' to undermine the USSR's economic autonomy, and finally Soviet power itself.

The weapon was also pointed towards the global South. In 1974 President Gerald Ford made a scarcely veiled threat to OPEC and other commodity-exporting countries in a speech at the UN General Assembly:

> All nations must seek to achieve a level of prices which not only provides an incentive to producers but which consumers can afford. . . . The attempt by any nation to use one commodity for political purposes will inevitably tempt other countries to use their commodities for their own purposes. . . . The United States recognizes the special responsibility we bear as the world's largest producer of food. . . . It has not been our policy to use food as a political weapon, despite the oil embargo and recent oil prices and production decisions.[8]

It has commonly been observed that successful development usually follows agricultural success. And, indeed, for several decades past both China and India have pursued resolute policies of food self-sufficiency. The case was argued thus in a book that compared China's economic reforms with those of the USSR under Gorbachev:

In the 1980s there was intense discussion among Chinese policy-makers about the degree to which the country could depend safely on world markets for food, especially grain... The government judged that there would be large risks involved in greater integration with world food markets, especially for a country of China's size and income level. . . .

This meant that the Chinese government needed to push and/or encourage China's farmers to grow more grain to maintain a higher degree of grain self-sufficiency than they would have done under free market conditions. This imposed high costs upon the Chinese economy. However, the government judged that the costs were worth bearing in reducing China's dependence on the international economy.[9]

This policy stood in sharp contrast to those of Khruschev and Brezhnev in the USSR, and it remains little changed even now. According to UNCTAD's statistics, in 2005 China exported more food than it imported (worth $24.6 billion compared with $21.5 billion) and food items accounted for only 3.3 per cent of its imports. Its imports of agricultural raw materials, on the other hand, were worth nearly six times its corresponding exports ($23.6 billion against $4.1 billion). But of the $138 billion increase in China's annual imports of primary commodities since 1995, $109 billion was in ores, metals and fuels.[10] Using different definitions, the FAO shows China as having had an $11.8 billion deficit in food trade in 2005, but $8.7 billion of this was accounted for by soya beans – not a staple food even in Chinese cuisine.[11]

On the other hand, in the same year Africa's net imports of wheat, rice and maize reached 55 million tons, just the same as the USSR's grain imports at their highest point. SSA's imports, net of exports, included 14.5 million tons of wheat, 11.4 million tons of rice and 854,000 tons of maize.[12] In general, the trade balances of poor countries in staple foods have seriously deteriorated since 1990. SSA has switched from being a net exporter to a net importer of cassava, maize, millet, sorghum and sugar, while its deficit in rice has more than doubled and its deficit in wheat has more than tripled; Table 7 gives details.[13] Small island states also tend to have high ratios

Table 7 Sub-Saharan Africa's trade in staple foods and sugar

		1990	2000	2005	% change, 1990–2005
Bananas	Production	5,549	5,935	6,680	+20
	Exports	282	458	513	
	Imports	34	80	71	
	Exports − imports	247	378	442	
Plantains	Production	18,889	21,567	23,387	+24
	Exports	1	1	1	
	Imports	0	1	1	
	Exports − imports	1	0	0	
Cassava, fresh and dried	Production	70,042	97,154	118,703	+69
	Exports	144	53	44	
	Imports	83	89	137	
	Exports − imports	61	−36	−93	
Maize	Production	32,600	38,208	42,985	+32
	Exports	3,906	1,154	2,939	
	Imports	2,226	1,703	3,793	
	Exports −imports	1,680	−549	−854	
Meat	Production	6,962	8,432	9,295	+34
	Exports	589	422	278	
	Imports	774	917	1,502	
	Exports − imports	−184	−495	−1,224	
Milk	Production	16,932	15,704	21,554	+27
	Exports	984	931	476	
	Imports	2,535	2,901	3,478	
	Exports − imports	−1,551	−1,971	−3,003	
Millet	Production	10,711	12,641	16,352	+53
	Exports	138	35	26	
	Imports	63	32	121	
	Exports − imports	75	3	−95	
Paddy rice	Production	9,198	11,049	13,626	+48
	Exports	288	242	637	
	Imports	4,945	7,349	11,987	
	Exports − imports	−4,658	−7,107	−11,351	
Pulses (total)	Production	6,084	7,834	9,869	+62
	Exports	230	118	273	
	Imports	238	306	537	
	Exports − imports	−8	−188	−263	

Table 7 cont.

		1990	2000	2005	% change, 1990—2005
Sorghum	Production	11,497	17,485	23,765	+107
	Exports	160	221	89	
	Imports	67	109	506	
	Exports − imports	93	112	−417	
Sugar crops	Production	56,870	66,481	69,738	+23
	Exports	21,783	23,245	23,213	
	Imports	16,711	22,311	34,381	
	Exports − imports	5,071	934	−11,168	
Sweet potatoes	Production	5,760	10,210	11,804	+105
	Exports	8	12	12	
	Imports	6	5	7	
	Exports − imports	3	7	5	
Vegetables	Production	17,877	24,335	27,577	+54
	Exports	472	443	467	
	Imports	817	1,339	2,470	
	Exports − imports	−345	−896	−2,003	
Wheat	Production	3,321	4,710	5,561	+67
	Exports	761	537	821	
	Imports	5,346	9,584	15,312	
	Exports − imports	−4,585	−9,047	−14,491	

Notes:
(1) Intra-SSA trade is included, but most root crops are excluded because of the small amounts traded.
(2) All figures are in thousands of metric tons.
(3) A nought (0) means less than 500 tons traded.
(4) The export and import data include both raw and processed forms, in primary equivalent totals.
(5) The export − import sums might not add up, because of rounding.

Source: FAOSTAT Database, «faostat.fao.org/site/336/DesktopDefault.aspx?PageID=336», October 2007.

of food imports to exports. Quite a few of them have been sheltered by preferential trade arrangements for bananas and sugar in the European Union and the US, but their fragile agricultural bases are now at risk as these preferences are being diluted or are about to be removed entirely. And despite imports, in some of the food-deficit countries very high levels of malnutrition are reported, reaching 67 per cent of the population in Burundi, 72 per cent in DR Congo and 73 per cent in Eritrea in 2001–3.[14]

These increasing food imports are perhaps the most telling indictment of the policies of 'accelerated development' adopted in the 1980s. Just as the Soviet Union discovered a quarter of a century ago, financing imports on such a scale is unsustainable. It renders impossible the international caution exhibited by both India and China and brings with it a huge political risk, as the warnings of Presidents Ford and Bush, some 27 years apart, and the fate suffered by the USSR all indicate. Consider the vulnerability of a small country like Djibouti in East Africa, as described in a recent report financed by George Bush's own US Administration:

> As Djibouti imports all its staple foods, most of [the] continuous increases in basic food commodity prices are due to influences outside of local markets. Some causes include the decreased harvest in wheat-producing areas in Australia, and the high value of the euro relative to the dollar.... Additionally, high fuel prices increase transport costs. Another important factor is the increased demand for grain and vegetable oil crops for the production of bio-fuels.... All these factors are significantly influencing the cost of the expenditure basket and thereby the food access of poor Djiboutian families.[15]

And all of them are well outside the Djibouti government's control. Another path needs urgently to be found, so that poor countries in Africa and elsewhere can avoid this source of vulnerability and use their scarce foreign currency earnings for economically constructive purposes rather than merely to feed their people – or, as argued in the case of the USSR, to finance the development of other countries' agriculture.

The roots of an answer

A greater range of staple foods is eaten in different parts of Africa than on other continents, and many of them are little traded internationally. Moreover, with the exception of wheat, all the staple foods consumed in Africa are widely grown on the continent itself: grains such as sorghum, millet, rice and maize; root crops including cassava, yams and sweet potatoes; and other types of food such as pulses, bananas and plantains, as well as meat and dairy products. Many of them are produced – and to a considerable extent placed on commercial markets – by smallholders who are among the poorest people on the continent. However, the countries of SSA imported $18.9 billion worth of food in 2005, and only $4.1 billion (22 per cent) of it was from each other.[16] The widening gap between food exports and imports is being filled by imports from developed countries or, in the case of rice, more prosperous developing countries in other regions. This cannot be sustained. Taken together, it adds up to intractable food insecurity, vulnerability and openness to foreign pressure – just what George Bush warned against for his own country. The lack of national and regional integration, coupled with the emphasis on global exports, has prevented Africa from controlling its food supplies for itself. It is urgent that we find measures to overcome this problem.

One set of circumstances, if combined properly, could contribute to an advance in welfare all round. Market opportunities could be expanded for many of the poorest rural people, while providing governments with an easier context in which to overcome other constraints on development. The first requirement is to stop farmers being displaced from their own national markets. Among other things, this means examining those staple crops that are produced or consumed (or both) by poor people, and which they find they can rely on the most, rather than those which could produce the greatest cash income if all goes well. The International Food Policy Research Institute (IFPRI) recently argued,

> The greatest market potential for most African farmers still lies in
> domestic and regional markets for food staples (cereals, roots and

tubers, pulses, oil crops, and livestock products). For Africa as a whole, the consumption of these commodities accounts for more than 70 per cent of agricultural output and is projected to double by 2015. This growth will add about US$50 billion per year to demand in 1996–2000 prices.... Moreover, with increasing commercialization and urbanization, much of this additional demand will translate into market transactions and not just additional on-farm consumption. No other agricultural markets could offer such growth potential and benefit to Africa's small farmers at such huge scales. Many small farms could significantly increase their incomes if they could capture a large share of this market growth.[17]

This does not apply only in Africa: it has been reported that, 'Supermarkets in Latin America buy 2.5 times more fruits and vegetables from local producers than all the exports of produce from Latin America to the rest of the world! *This should be contrasted with the nearly-exclusive focus on produce exports in government and donor programs.*'[18] And despite the scale of imports, staple food production has already been Africa's great unnoticed success story of recent years. As can be seen in Table 7, SSA's production of sorghum and sweet potatoes has doubled since 1990 while that of cassava, millet, pulses and vegetables has risen by more than half, according to the FAO's statistics. In most of these crops there is very little international trade. Much of the increase, especially in root crops, occurred in Nigeria, where production of cassava, plantains, pulses, sorghum and vegetables all more than doubled between 1990 and 2005, while yam output went up by 150 per cent to reach 34 million tons.

This did not happen by accident. Nigeria was a successful participant in a recent programme called the Global Cassava Development Strategy (GCDS), led by the FAO and IFAD. With demand for staple foods growing due to increases in population, this programme has used various means to promote the use of cassava as a traditional staple crop which suits local needs well. In some countries farmers were encouraged to grow cassava by indirect policies. Nigeria, which produces more than one-third of Africa's crop, followed an idea pioneered in Brazil: the mandatory inclusion of 10 per cent cassava flour in bread and confectionery products.[19] Across Africa, the measures have included the development of new cassava varieties, and found incidental support in policies for certain other crops:

> Cassava production has grown rapidly across the cassava belt of East and Southern Africa over the past two decades. A stream of new varietal releases from the International Institute of Tropical Agriculture has triggered a surge in cassava productivity, while the dismantling of widespread maize subsidies, in the early 1990s, has reinforced farmer incentives to diversify out of maize production.[20]

We saw in Chapter 3 how much Nigeria has expanded its production of vegetables (and thereby reduced its import bill), and it has done the same for cassava and several other staple foods. But Nigeria has never been one of the nations singled out by the development establishment for praise. On the contrary, it has been rather scorned: from 1993 to 1999 the World Bank refused even to lend it any new money. That establishment, led by the Bank, likes to spotlight a country or two that are considered to pursue model policies for others to follow. A quarter of a century ago, the West African favourite was Côte d'Ivoire, which had diversified its commodity exports under President Félix Houphouët-Boigny. In more recent times other countries such as Uganda and Ghana have played the part – in spite of the disastrous surge of food imports in Ghana under its trade liberalization policies.

Nigeria remains a major food importer, but its development of cassava and other domestic food production has achieved better results in recent years than its neighbours. Its successes have not been haphazard but were in good part a result of considered government policies. But they went against current fashion because they were largely about substituting for imports rather than building up exports (of which Nigeria has plenty in its oil). However, it was Nigeria's imports (of beans and onions, for example) from its African neighbours that declined, while its imports of staple foods from outside Africa increased; many of them, such as wheat and rice, were subsidized by the main exporting countries. It remains to be seen what effect the doubling of world wheat prices in 2007 will have on this pattern, but policy initiatives of this sort need to be better coordinated between neighbouring countries to ensure that all benefit from them.

Yet despite these successes, we find that an official evaluation of the World Bank's assistance to African agriculture criticized 'a lack of appreciation ... for the important role of cassava and other root crops in providing food security'. It pointed out that the Bank was not even a member of the GCDS consortium and ventured to provide a possible reason: 'Many Western food analysts still consider cassava as an inferior food whose *per capita* consumption is expected to decline with increasing *per capita* incomes, and it is possible that the Bank approach has been influenced by this thinking.'[21] We saw earlier that the Bank implicitly criticized sweet potatoes (preferred by poor farmers in Tanzania) as a 'low-value, low-return' root crop. But 'superior' foods originating on other continents, such as wheat and rice, are instrumental in the food trade crisis facing African countries, and the Bank's sort of thinking must be abandoned in favour of what can be shown to work for food supplies and poor rural people's incomes.

In India a somewhat comparable advance was achieved through the production of milk, distributed by cooperatives. Four decades after the experiment began, India has some 117,575 village dairy cooperatives and the livestock sector contributes more than one-quarter of agricultural output. Dairy products account for 70 per cent of that and provide employment for around 75 million women and 15 million men. India became self-sufficient in milk in 1993 and is now the largest producer of milk in the world. It is reported that almost 55 per cent of the milk produced is consumed by the producer households; of the remainder, 'Two-thirds is sold in informal markets and 15–16 per cent of the total milk produced in the country enters the organized market comprising cooperatives and the private sector.'[22] As a measure of the impact on poverty, 90 per cent of Indian rural households have less than two hectares of land or none at all, and between them they own three-quarters of the country's livestock; almost half of this class's income comes from livestock.[23]

Cattle are also an important asset as well as a source of food for many of the poorest communities in Africa, especially in the savannah areas which are scattered from Mali in the west to Kenya in the east and Botswana in the south. However, rather than this potential having been built on, perhaps using a variant of the Indian cooperative model, we find that SSA's net imports of milk nearly doubled from 1.6 million tons in 1990 to 3.0 million tons (or 14 per cent of SSA's production) in 2005.[24] This illustrates the inability to grow enough food to feed the people, of which President Bush spoke. And this is what has to change.

However, there is a further dilemma here. The growth in Africa's agricultural production has been achieved mostly through extensive development, based on expanded land use rather than higher crop yields. But this adds to environmental risks:

> In most cases production gains are coming about as a result of placing increasing amounts of land under cultivation rather than through the use of intensive technologies or varieties that can improve yields. . . . For cereals such as millet and sorghum ... production is expanding onto fragile lands, such as those in the Sahel that are already under severe risk of desertification.[25]

But there is plenty of potential to expand yields without falling prey to the alternative predator of environmental damage arising from excessive use of agricultural chemicals.

The regional option

It is timely to ask how much good it will do to integrate poor food-deficit countries even more tightly into global markets. Arguably, at independence the former European colonies were *too* integrated in the global economy; priority should have been given to developing *national* economic integration and *regional* trade. Robert Wade has argued:

> One of the strangest silences of development thinking is the silence about internal integration. We should distinguish between 'external integration' and 'internal integration' ... and recognize that the

development of a national economy is more about internal integration than about external integration. . . .

Development strategy has to operate in the zone where the two forms of integration reinforce rather than undermine each other. But the fact is that the issues of internal integration – including practical nuts-and-bolts issues like nurturing supply links between domestic firms and the subsidiaries of multinational corporations ... – have largely dropped out of the development agenda as promulgated by Western development organizations.[26]

In this regard, it is important that rural policy should start not with foreign trade but with food security. In recent times, better ideas in this area have come from organizations concerned with food than from those that deal with general development and poverty reduction. Examples are IFAD and IFPRI. Their concerns are to identify what forms of agriculture and agricultural trade most directly benefit the poorest rural people, and I share those concerns. It happens that the potential for agriculture is strong in a continent like Africa, which has vast natural resources and demand for 880 million people to be fed. African countries need more food, and market demands for food will continue to grow. But it also contains unorganized, underdeveloped and incomplete markets, inadequate commercial institutions and disruptions in price transmission between different market levels and regions.

Africa's economic systems were formed in colonial times to supply European markets, and mostly they remain directed towards other continents. Not only do many of their domestic economies lack integration, but the links with their closest neighbours are also attenuated. For example, in some cases telephone connections between neighbouring capitals in West Africa still go via London and Paris, the former colonial capitals. It should have been a major task of development ever since decolonization to build up the domestic and regional linkages, since the links with global markets were already quite highly developed. But this was not done during the 1960s and 1970s, and after that it was ruled out by the push for integration in the world economy and exports to *global* markets.

Continental integration was part of the Lagos Plan in 1980 but it was pushed aside by the Berg Report and structural adjustment, as we saw in Chapter 2. Since then international policy has insisted on global integration as an absolute priority; indeed, in the case of such institutions as agricultural marketing boards, it even required elements of internal integration that already existed to be destroyed rather than improved and built upon.

An expansion of regional trade, as was envisaged in the Lagos Plan, could be of great benefit to Africa's smallholders and agricultural workers. Regional markets composed of several countries can develop economies of scale, which, as we saw in the Chinese and Indian cases, are vitally important for success in modern world trade. This could be achieved at a level of technology in products – as well as logistical, managerial and marketing skills – consistent with that of Africa's producers. This marks a sharp contrast with the stringent demands of technology, product standards and capital which are made on agriculturalists in the integrated global supply chains of today. It also carries more promise for poverty reduction and balanced prosperity than relying on exports to new foreign markets such as China, promising though these are in certain cases. But it does require concentrated political attention and careful planning, such as lay behind the development successes of Japan and China, or – nearer home – Mauritius and Botswana.

The general aim is to enable food-surplus regions to meet the needs of food-deficit regions of the continent more easily, leading to benefits for both. As a recent paper for the Common Market for Eastern and Southern Africa (COMESA) argued: 'Africa's hunger hot spots are well known.... Less well advertised are a series of highly productive, regularly surplus food production zones across Africa.' It suggested that when hunger hot spots face shortfalls, farmers from nearby surplus zones should be 'able to harvest more of their perennial reserve crops (cassava or bananas) and in turn free up more cereals (primarily maize) for export to deficit zones.'[27] This process will have to be helped along if such surpluses are to be sustained and built up over the long term:

Failure to facilitate expansion of national and regional trade in food staples risks stalling production growth and private investment in agriculture. In thin national markets, without export outlets, production surges lead easily to price collapses, such as that witnessed in Ethiopia during the 2001/2 season. In turn, these disincentives dampen long-term agricultural income growth.[28]

IFPRI too has concluded that better integration of regional markets could provide important outlets for increased grain production in some countries. Some intra-African trade of this sort already occurs, on both formal and informal markets, for example in maize in East and Southern Africa.[29] Indeed, in the 1996–2000 period, staple cereals including maize comprised the largest element of intra-SSA agricultural trade, amounting to one-sixth of the total.[30] More than half of SSA's maize imports over that period came from other SSA countries, mostly within the same sub-region as the importing country.[31] There is also significant trade in sorghum, millet and livestock within West Africa, mainly in exports from the Sahelian to coastal countries. However, we saw in Chapter 3 that Niger's valuable exports of vegetables to Nigeria have fallen sharply, in part because of increasing domestic production of substitute crops and imports from elsewhere to Nigeria, but apparently also because of growing domestic consumption in Niger.

This trade is inhibited by poor roads, border restrictions, currency problems and numerous other handicaps. It needs to be deliberately coaxed. The lack of sufficiently developed commercial and administrative institutions needs to be addressed at the national, regional and international levels. The problems of communications require appropriate prioritization of public expenditure. There is a widespread view that one of the keys to agricultural and rural development in underdeveloped regions lies in building roads and other infrastructure, as China has done. Yet it is interesting that Brazil's success in agricultural exports has come despite what has been described as a 'shaky infrastructure', with just 10 per cent of the country's roads paved.[32] In agricultural trade, another obstacle lies in the bulkiness or perishability of many staple foods, especially root crops and some coarse grains such as millet. Agronomic research needs to be expanded and upgraded to find ways of overcoming this.

Different food staples prevail in different parts of the continent, such as maize in Southern Africa, bananas in parts of East Africa, and sorghum, millet, cassava and livestock products in various parts of West Africa. Production capacities and consumption needs vary within the sub-regions; in many cases food production and consumption complement each other among the countries of a sub-region, or between regions or population groups within a country – for example, cereals and other staple crops such as beans grown by farmers, and livestock products among pastoralists. Given the communications difficulties and other transaction costs between African countries, there is generally more staple-food trade within a sub-region than between sub-regions of the continent; and it is more feasible to build on that.

However, support for trade in basic food commodities should have a greater impact than present policies do in the reduction of poverty. Much evidence suggests it is what happens in rural areas that matters most, at least in the early stages of development; to quote one piece of research:

> Using panel data from India for 1951 to 1990, Ravallion and Datt (1996) found ... that ... while urban growth reduced urban poverty, its effect was not significantly different from zero in explaining the rate of poverty reduction nationally. On the other hand, rural growth reduced poverty in rural and urban areas and hence had a significant, positive effect on national poverty reduction.[33]

Earlier we saw that many rural development thinkers have begun to question the prospects for small-scale farming; but the FAO still emphasizes the central place of smallholders in rural communities:

> Improving the productivity of small farmers has a ripple effect that spreads benefits throughout poor rural communities. When small farmers have more money to spend, they tend to spend it locally on labour-intensive goods and services that come from the rural non-farm sector, boosting the incomes of the rural population as a

whole, including landless labourers who make up a large part of the population of the poor and hungry in many countries.[34]

Here we see the opposite force to the fashionable trickle-down theory of income growth: structural change and development rising from below, or washing in from the rural margins. To assist it, it will be necessary to concentrate on building up domestic markets by such means as providing sources of credit and transport links in remote areas. Poor rural people's low capacity to diversify will have to be overcome: getting out of reliance on a narrow source of income or exports means widening the range, so that if the price of one falls it will not have such a severe effect on earnings as a whole. But this generally requires capital to invest as well as an ability to acquire the knowledge to produce the new product to the required standard. All of this is less readily available in poor countries, especially when the real prices of existing produce have themselves fallen. So it needs official, institutional support; the development of wider domestic and regional markets can play a large part in this.

The proposal matches the economic potential of African farmers, including subsistence farmers who have surpluses for sale. This type of trade exploits the very strengths of poorer and smaller farms, works with the grain of comparative advantage, and is more promising than the unequal trade patterns that pertain in both traditional and 'non-traditional' export commodities. Moreover, in recent decades international trade has not been conducted on the whole between countries with complementary economies, as the orthodox theory of comparative advantage would suggest, but between countries with similar characteristics at similar levels of development. When he formulated the theory of comparative advantage in the early nineteenth century, David Ricardo illustrated it with an example of trade between two countries that happened to have very different levels of development at the time: England, exporting cotton goods which were at the cutting edge of the new manufacturing technology, and agrarian Portugal, exporting a tradi-tionally processed agricultural product, wine. The overwhelming majority of recent world trade has been carried out among the

developed countries of the Organization for Economic Cooperation and Development, often exchanging similar products with
each other.

Indeed, one of the greatest success stories has been the economic
integration of the European Union, built on a free-trade zone in one
region between highly advanced economies with a common
external tariff, often at high duty rates. This model should be
applicable at lower levels of development, too, and it needs to be
unambiguously permitted there under WTO rules – including high
external tariffs where required. The approach is perhaps more
suitable than anywhere else in places where there is severe national
fragmentation, such as Africa. As one commentary put it:

> More than any other continent it is a patchwork of generally small
> nation states, most composed of different ethnic groups, each with
> their own history and culture. Different colonial histories have led
> to further diversity in institutions, language, culture, economic
> structure and trading patterns.[35]

In Europe, a somewhat comparable fragmentation led to two
continent-wide wars in the first half of the twentieth century.
Fortunately the situation in Africa has not descended to that level!
But Europe has overcome it over the last 50 years with a programme of gradual economic integration, achieved through careful
– if often difficult – intergovernmental negotiations. That is what
the countries of Africa themselves wanted to achieve under the
Lagos Plan, but the World Bank prevented it.

Similar benefits might also be generated for industry, providing a
way for countries to diversify into manufactures without having to
meet the strict demands made of exports to developed countries.
In parts of the developing world, international cooperation has
already helped to overcome commodity dependency. Besides
regional groupings such as the Association of South-East Asian
Nations and Mercosur in Latin America, there have been more
informal instances. For example, Bangladesh's expansion of garment
production in the 1980s was partly achieved through collaboration
with East Asian entrepreneurs, whose access to developed

countries was restricted at the time by trade quotas under the Multi-Fibre Arrangement.[36] In this way Bangladesh was able to overcome its dependence on the declining world market for jute. And in the case of a country which has been successful in *agricultural* exports to the developed world, in 2003 fully 67 per cent of Kenya's exports of manufactures (excluding agro-processed products) went to the 20-country regional market of COMESA, and only 9 per cent to the EU.[37] Largely in consequence of these manufactured exports, COMESA is now Kenya's leading export destination, taking 36.6 per cent of its 2005 exports, with 25.4 per cent going to the EU in second place.[38]

After making due allowance for the different development levels, the pursuit of this goal in COMESA and other regional groupings would follow quite closely the European model of industrial integration since the 1960s. Among the current obstacles to regional trade is the lack of standardized packing, grading and quality-control systems.[39] 'Harmonization' of these standards was an important instrument of integration within the European Economic Community in its early days between the 1960s and 1980s. But one of the merits of the plan proposed here is that it need not be done at such advanced standards as was the case then, let alone those required to gain access to the European markets of today. Developing-country manufacturers could then eventually compete on the world stage after the barriers were taken down. It has after all been argued that

> The nature of technical progress and new technology is heavily biased in favour of skilled and educated labour, as technical change emanates from [research and development] activities in the developed (industrialized) countries in response to local conditions. Hence, technical change tends to be labour-saving and skill-biased, and new technology is complementary to capital and skilled labour, while it is a substitute for unskilled labour and tends to increase inequalities in both developed and developing countries.[40]

This is clearly contrary to the needs of the poorest developing countries. But in China, small-scale township and village enterprises (TVEs), using local technologies, were widely credited with much of the early dynamism of the industrialization drive. The present plan would also enable industries to develop with a sufficient scale in a relatively large 'home' market, coming as close as could be achieved to replicating China's and India's pattern of gradually fostering industrial development by the use of locally generated capital behind protective trade barriers. However, the growth of non-farm rural jobs, even in TVEs, depends to a large extent on the vitality of the *farm* economy; the agricultural and non-agricultural sectors are mutually supporting.

There are high barriers to trade both within countries and between neighbouring countries in many parts of SSA. Tariffs are often higher between neighbouring African countries than between them and countries in the developed world. In many cases, there is also insufficient macroeconomic compatibility between countries within a regional bloc. For example, effective trade integration is usually best assisted by a regional currency reference, rather than defining each currency separately against the currencies of the rich world. Confusion is also induced by the proliferation of regional groupings, with overlapping memberships and sometimes conflicting principles of cooperation. Between them, the 30 continental African LDCs are members of 13 different intra-African regional trade arrangements; 11 countries appear to be members of three or more of them at once. This needs to be simplified and rationalized, preferably under the auspices of the African Union. Yet there is also a danger that the EU's own proposed new trade agreements with African, Caribbean and Pacific countries (the Economic Partnership Agreements), far from supporting regional integration efforts as intended, might actually undermine them. In any case, any Southern regional trade group which includes a powerful Northern bloc like the EU would necessarily run counter to the needs of integration that we are discussing.

The global dimension

Just as there has been some reawakening of awareness in the last few years about the problems posed by commodity export markets, so the questions of domestic and regional integration have also aroused new interest. UNCTAD has observed:

> African LDCs have undertaken deeper and faster trade liberalization than Asian LDCs. But it is the latter that have generally had a better performance in terms of poverty reduction and also have been more successful in developing more market-dynamic manufactures exports, *partly through regional trade and investment linkages.*[41]

There has been some recent attention from researchers and, to a degree, donors and policy makers to the 'incompleteness' of markets in poor countries, especially in rural areas and for rural products. This is related to the concept of economic integration, but it is not identical. It is usually understood in the context of enabling a country's rural areas to react appropriately to price signals that arrive from global markets. As this book has argued, too close an attachment to global markets is a source of instability and weakness in developing countries, especially the poorest of them. However, many of the usual prescriptions on incomplete markets should be pursued, for example building infrastructure, facilitating credit and promoting commercial institutions, including those with neighbouring countries and in sub-regions. However, rather than being a means of facilitating open links with world markets, for the foreseeable future these domestic and regional developments should be *protected* wherever required from the harmful influences of external commerce. Domestic and regional integration, and the upgrading of incomplete markets, cannot work without the global measures discussed in previous chapters of this book.

Some of these ideas have reached some agents who have influence over current events, and advocates of the approach suggested here can appeal to such agents, as Michigan State University does in this passage:

> Very much in the spirit of NEPAD [the New Partnership for Africa's Development], this initiative seeks to build on Africa's strengths to develop sustainable solutions to Africa's key problems. In a cohesive structural way, it directly contributes to the expansion of domestic and sub-regional markets (CAADP Pillar #2). It

likewise promotes improved food security and food production (Pillar #3).[42]

As far as it goes, this is encouraging, but the approach will have only limited success as long as the attitudes to global markets discussed elsewhere in this book remain unchanged. If these initiatives are pursued alone and the global constraints on development are not addressed, it will be yet another example of blaming the poor for their poverty and ignoring the global conditions that create and reinforce it. All approaches to the problem need to be pursued and they will reinforce each other. They include domestic and regional integration in areas that will be of the greatest and most direct benefit to the poorest in society, fundamental reform of the commodity markets, and the development of global competition policy to tackle concentrations of corporate power.

Notes

1   White House (2001).
2   See Table 7 in this chapter and FAO, «faostat.fao.org/site/336/Desktop Default.aspx?PageID=336» (November 2007).
3   Jasny (1951).
4   Gaidar (2007), p. 2.
5   NACLA (1975), pp. 8 and 16.
6   *Business America* (1985).
7   Volkogonov (1995), p. 339.
8   Speech downloaded from «www.ford.utexas.edu/LIBRARY/speeches/740081.htm» (October 2007).
9   Nolan (1995), pp. 183–4.
10 UNCTAD, «stats.unctad.org/Handbook/TableViewer/tableView.aspx?ReportId=1299» (November 2007).
11 FAO,   «faostat.fao.org/site/336/DesktopDefault.aspx?PageID=336» (November 2007).
12 *Ibid.*
13 Country-by-country data can be found at the FAO's FAOSTAT database: «faostat.fao.org/faostat/collections?version=ext&hasbulk=0&subset=agriculture» (October 2007).
14 Deutscher Welthungerhilfe *et al.* (2007), Appendix C, pp. 52–3.

15 FEWS NET (2007a).

16 Data from UNCTAD *Handbook of Statistics 2006*, viewed at «stats.unctad.org./Handbook/TableViewer/tableView.aspx».

17 Diao *et al.* (2007), p. 17.

18 Reardon *et al.* (2003b), p. 8 (emphasis in the original).

19 FAO (2007), p. 16.

20 COMESA and Michigan State University (undated), p. 4.

21 Independent Evaluation Group (2007), p. 52, Box 5.2.

22 Goswami (2007), p. 3.

23 *Ibid.*, pp. 2–4.

24 FAO, «faostat.fao.org/site/336/DesktopDefault.aspx?PageID=336» (November 2007).

25 PriceWaterhouseCoopers (2005), p. 67.

26 Wade (2005), p. 94.

27 COMESA and Michigan State University (undated), p. 1.

28 *Ibid.*, p. 2.

29 See, for example, FEWS NET (2007b) and «www.fews.net/monthlies», *passim*.

30 Diao *et al.* (2003), p. 12, Table 5.

31 *Ibid.*, p. 31.

32 *The Economist* (2005).

33 Diao *et al.* (2007), Box 2.5, p. 11, citing Ravallion and Datt (1996).

34 FAO (2004b), p. 32.

35 Kydd *et al.* (2002), p. 13.

36 Hossain (1990), p. 4.

37 EcoNews Africa (2005), p. 2, citing Ihiga (2005).

38 Republic of Kenya (2007), p. 4.

39 FAO (2004a), pp. 28–9.

40 Nissanke and Thorbecke (2007), p. 231.

41 UNCTAD (2004), p. viii (emphasis added).

42 COMESA and Michigan State University (undated), p. 5.

6
Can we put history behind us?

The history of globalization

Globalization is often described as though it was a force of nature, which has appeared without any human intervention and which no human intervention can influence; all we can do is adapt to it. There are some elements of the process that are not a direct result of policy, such as the technologies that have led to faster travel and closer communications around the world. But the economic aspects of globalization arise directly from policy. They are the consequence of decisions made by governments over the last 25 to 30 years, and such decisions can be reversed as easily as they were made.

It has often been remarked that there was a previous era of globalization, in which the world economy was almost as integrated as today and international trade represented almost as large a share of world output. That era was a hundred years ago, running from the late nineteenth century until the outbreak of the First World War in 1914. It coincided with the era of European high imperialism. In much of Europe it was accepted as normal that people from that continent could go to other continents not just to trade, but to conquer and rule the territories and peoples. In the great imperial countries, and most of all the United Kingdom, this was curiously aligned with the high moral tone of the Victorian era. While British railwaymen were building stations and track for profit in India and Argentina, and Cecil Rhodes was digging for gold and diamonds in Southern Africa, many of their compatriots sincerely regarded the imperial venture as a 'civilizing mission', in which it was necessary to 'take up the white man's burden' in those distant lands. This was not merely a hypocritical façade: Victorian morality did lead many men and women to settle in uncomfortable and unfamiliar surroundings and set up religious missions, establish hospitals or devise alphabets for languages that did not have them before. The modern concept of 'humanitarian' military intervention descends from the same tradition.

The first era of globalization collapsed in the long series of European catastrophes of the First World War, the 1929 stock market crash, mass unemployment during the Great Depression, and then the fascist era and further abominations in the Second World War. And there was a popular revolt against capitalism itself, seen in the socialist revolution in Russia and the development of trade unions and socialist and Communist parties across the industrial world. When the Second World War ended in 1945 there was a deep feeling of 'never again': the Depression, preceded by the speculative crash on the stock markets and followed by the genocide of the Jews, was associated in many minds with a failure of *laissez-faire* capitalism, and a more humane economic model was set up for the post-war world. International finance was to be stabilized by the IMF, the World Bank would help countries to reconstruct and develop after the ravages of war, and domestic policy would harness the forces of the market for the wider good of the people. In the international sphere, disputes would be regulated through the United Nations, and the European powers would decolonize, at last realizing former US President Woodrow Wilson's concept of the self-determination of nations.

In the industrial countries' domestic policy, the main economic goal was to maintain full employment, supported by a welfare state, progressive taxation of higher incomes at higher rates than lower ones, and the public ownership of basic parts of the economy such as the mines, the steel, electricity and gas industries, the railways and telephone systems, and in some countries the banks. A notable feature of the period throughout the developed world was a gradual reduction of domestic income differentials.

However, the 'beggar-my-neighbour' policies of the 1930s had led the industrial countries away from world markets, and so each country by 1945 had its own national markets and domestic companies which supplied them, protected from competition by import tariffs. Where a country had colonies and other overseas associates, these privileges were extended to them, most importantly in the UK's system of Empire and Commonwealth preference and the Sterling currency area. In time another group of countries developed a common market with common external tariffs, after the European Economic Community was set up in 1957. Meanwhile, under the GATT industrial tariffs were progressively reduced in order to promote trade between these capitalist fortresses; but interventionist, state-subsidized agricultural policies were exempted from it in order to ensure the revival of agricultural output in the developed world, and so was the trade in textiles because of the fear of imports from poorer countries.

After decolonization, the newly independent countries soon found that economic power was still unequal between them and their former colonial rulers, and political independence was not enough. Complaints about economic neo-colonialism led in the 1970s to demands to establish a New International Economic Order, a central feature of which was to be an Integrated Programme for Commodities that UNCTAD set out to negotiate, with a view to establishing stable and remunerative prices for commodity exports.

However, there was a reaction against most of these policies in the industrial world from the late 1970s on, starting with the election in 1979 of a Conservative government in the UK. The government was pledged to return to the policies of the free market, as recommended by the *laissez-faire* theories of neo-classical economics. Before long these began to be imposed on much of the rest of the world, using the leverage afforded to the IMF and the World Bank by the international debt crisis of the 1980s. New policies on trade, patents, investment rules and many other matters were entrenched when the GATT was transformed into the WTO after the Uruguay Round of trade negotiations, which began in 1986. And so we come to structural adjustment and its aftermath, which this book has already examined.

New directions

There have been suggestions that new market opportunities will overcome many of the problems we have discussed. Most prominently, there has been new trade and investment interest, especially from China, in the supply of minerals and agricultural raw materials. However, so far this has been little reflected in demand for food crops, and China still imports little of the traditional tropical food commodities such as coffee and bananas. But the new demand for oil and metals is a great help to certain countries that have the natural resources required, such as Angola.

There has also been growth in recent years of so-called South–South trade between developing countries. This has led to more complex trading patterns, away from a narrow dependence on European, North American and Japanese markets and their transnational corporations (TNCs). It has been of undoubted economic benefit for countries to diversify their trading partners and sources of foreign investment, and there have been political consequences too. The loosening of commercial dependence on the US has enabled Latin America to pursue more independent domestic policies and even to start to break with the IMF and the World Bank – with Venezuela, Bolivia and, more recently, Ecuador in the vanguard. But in agriculture the structural deficiencies of global trade will surely re-emerge with new trading partners, unless other policy measures are brought in to inhibit them.

There has also been rising worldwide demand for crops from which to make ethanol and other biofuels, such as sugar cane and palm oil. It is not yet clear how much this will help the poorest countries. Most of them are a long distance from the main fuel markets and it has been estimated that the savings in carbon emissions will be small or negative, after inputs required for production and carriage have been netted out.[1] It will also provide competition for land that is currently used for food. However, it has given a boost to the prices of some crops, such as maize. In the long run this should assist farmers' incomes in maize-producing areas in East and Southern Africa, among others.

However, it remains abundantly clear that a new policy mix is required. Six main lines of policy were put forward in this book, and they are summarized below.

1. Restore governments' power to determine their own policies

Since the turn of the millennium, the Post-Washington Consensus has modified the policies of structural adjustment and IMF conditionality, but it has not changed their essentials. Moreover, they have been reinforced by the requirements of the WTO, including the Agreement on Agriculture which comes under it. But national governments are the best placed to determine policy for their countries. That is, after all, why Europe's former colonies sought and won their independence a generation or two ago. It is time that international agencies, and the rich countries' governments, stopped interfering in developing countries' economic policies, including the most fundamental of all, those for food and agriculture.

2. End any requirement for export orientation

This is a corollary of the first recommendation. As a universal policy requirement, export orientation has clearly failed. Great vulnerability can arise from foreign trade in poor countries. Much of this is due to the volatility and unreliability of the export markets on which they depend, as we have seen. A guiding aim should be to use trade and market-development policies to enable small farmers to find markets for their produce at a technological level that suits their capabilities, and use their capacity to produce staple foods as the means to feed growing populations and reduce food import bills. But this is not proposed as a universal dogma: if a country sees fit to base its policies on an export strategy, it must be free to do so. In some circumstances this undoubtedly works: for example, in Singapore, a small island state which had served in colonial times as an entrepôt on busy sea routes, the creation of export processing zones was a natural extension of the economic tradition and it served the country well. However, for many other countries quite different strategies are more suitable.

3. Restore international prices for agricultural products

This underpins everything else because of the commodity basis of the poorest countries' economies, and its rural links to the greatest poverty. Items 1, 2 and 4 on this list should go a long way towards achieving this goal, but direct interventions are also needed. Whatever means can be found should be used to cut back oversupplies and guarantee export markets, and exporting countries should be able to manage their production and exports cooperatively, wherever it is feasible. Trade should be managed in a broad range of export commodities, especially those of developing countries at the lower end of the scale, for example through the use of export or import quotas to major markets. This will help the markets to function better as markets and provide a counterweight to concentrations of market power. It will bring to poor countries the sort of public advantage that Mauritius has derived from its guaranteed sugar import quota in the EU, or the commercial advantage that Botswana derives from its diamond export arrangement with the De Beers company's Central Selling Organization. In spite of recent increases in many agricultural prices, including latterly for cereals, such arrangements are an important requirement for *developed countries'* farmers too.

4. Restore the balance of power along international supply chains

In an era of global markets, corporations must be regulated at the global level. This requires the reduction of concentrations of corporate power by various means, including in certain circumstances the break-up of corporations and oligopsonies at the national or global levels. One recent study reached this conclusion: 'While dismantling corporations may seem like the most difficult solution to the corporate domination which is causing the farming crisis, it is the only solution in our view that will realistically make space needed for creating a truly democratic food system.'[2] That study was of British agriculture but the conclusion applies all the more strongly to farming in weaker and more vulnerable countries. It has been proposed that there should be a maximum size limit for corporations. This is not the place to decide on the details of such a scheme, but it could be based on the market shares held by individual companies or dominant groups of them.

Meanwhile, at the producers' end of the supply chain other means also need to be used to rebalance economic power. One of them is to enforce strictly the requirement under international law for all countries to comply with all International Labour Organization labour standards that they have ratified; many of these are of great importance for agricultural workers.

5. Support domestic agriculture and the production of staple foods

The first goal of rural policies should be to make sure that both rural and urban people have enough to eat. This is the goal of food security. There is a well-known group of policies which enabled West European countries to boost agricultural output and income from the 1950s until the 1980s: they included guaranteed prices, subsidies, marketing boards, domestic supply management, import tariffs and quotas. That is not a prescription for developing countries' policies, but they should be free to choose any or all of the above as they see fit. For history shows that development success is associated with domestic control over food supplies and a lack of dependence on food imports. It is dangerous for a government to lack control over food policy, as we saw in the case of Djibouti where all staple foods are imported. By contrast, both India and China have over the last 40 years aimed at food self-sufficiency; together with their lack of foreign debts, this gave them the freedom they needed to determine their own lines of development.

Policy must ensure that there are sufficient supplies of a country's main staple foods. Domestic supply management deserves to be considered, with the proviso that it requires adequately high import tariffs (or restrictive import quotas) to make it work. Additional requirements are agronomic and marketing advice, and the strengthening of provisions such as roads and transport. These policies need to be supported by more agricultural research into traditional staple foods.

6. Promote domestic and regional trade, especially in staple foods
For most poor countries domestic and regional market integration needs to be prioritized above global integration. Food security should be emphasized above trade in general. This would facilitate the supply of food from surplus areas to places of food shortage and hunger. An important channel will be to build up regional trade links, especially where there are many poor countries with contiguous borders, many of these countries being small in size; that means in Africa above all. Regional arrangements should be strengthened and rationalized to generate regional trade, providing the same benefits to neighbours at similar levels of development as Europe has achieved over the last 50 years, and the best available substitute for the national economies of scale enjoyed by India and China.

Unmaking poverty

This book started with the questions of what *made* poverty and *why* poor people are poor. These are complex questions and there is no simple or obvious set of answers. However, I have argued that the present emphasis on internal arrangements within developing countries, including their political systems, provides at best a partial answer. Meanwhile, the insistence on integration with world markets and the privileging of international trade and exports has proved very damaging, at any rate for the poorest and weakest countries. We saw that in past times similar policies were closely linked with economic imperialism. The last era of globalization coincided with the heyday of European worldwide empires, while before that the markets of India, China and other countries were forced open for manufactured imports from the colonial powers. Many fine craft traditions were destroyed in the process.

We observed in Chapter 1 that in the current era of globalization most of the poorest countries' economies had stagnated, many had grown substantially poorer and their levels of development had been reduced – at a time when the countries of the rich world prospered as never before. Then in Chapter 2 we saw that Guy Gran in 1982 described the Berg Report on 'Accelerated Development' as 'a study of what African governments should do to promote Western capital'.[3] Many later commentators have seen it in the same light, but it is interesting to see that this was already understood at the time. Writing as a witness from one of the world's rich nations, it is hard not to feel angry with these policies that were imposed on the people of developing countries. The widening gap between rich and poor countries has made it even more difficult for the poor to catch up with the rich world, partly because of the huge technological gulf that now lies between them. The very dynamism of the market economy, if not properly harnessed, leads to poverty being *made*.

In the early period after decolonization the countries of the developing world united in pursuit of policies that would suit them better collectively. However, during the debt crisis those aspirations were crushed and new, less favourable arrangements were installed in their place. The rhetoric of globalization implies that there is nothing we can do now to alter these arrangements: they are here to stay and seemingly immutable. The mainstream development debate now revolves largely around how to enable developing countries to make the most of this framework.

But the framework itself is faulty. It is, above all, economic characteristics that are shared by the dozens of countries that have fallen behind under globalization: small size, remoteness and a dependence on agriculture, commodity exports and food imports. The deepest poverty is in rural areas, and even fast-growing countries like China and India, as well as many countries of the rich world, face a rural crisis. For the very poorest countries, the dogma of export orientation has exacerbated these problems, with a sharp decline in the real prices of many of the very exports that were meant to be their salvation. Until the world seriously addresses these global factors, there will be little hope of substantially narrowing the economic gap.

This indeed is the background to the stalemate between developed and developing countries which has bedevilled trade negotiations ever since the WTO's aborted conference in Seattle in 1999. The rhetoric behind the WTO's Doha Round, when it started in the Qatari capital in 2001, was to give priority to development. It was even officially titled the Doha Development Round, in an implicit recognition that the current rules do not best suit the needs of development. The developing countries required this change of emphasis after the fiasco in Seattle. But it has been undermined, yet again, by the persistent bullying and manipulation of the negotiations by the minority of rich countries, and especially the most powerful of them.[4]

All of this poses a huge dilemma. Should we continue to take the present arrangements for agriculture and trade as the starting point, and insist that the poorest rural people find ways to fit in with them? This book has argued that we should not. We should insist instead on giving priority to the needs and interests of 900 million poor people in rural areas, and seek ways for the rest of us to accommodate *them*. In the economic sphere, their most important needs are adequate wages for workers' labour and adequate prices for farmers' produce. Under present market-dominated arrangements it could seem ambitious and even idealistic to set a goal of consistently meeting these needs. But those arrangements themselves represent a political choice. Other arrangements have existed before, and we can change the arrangements again. Considering the bleak future that so many people might otherwise face, this approach is the only humane one and it has to be pursued, in the face of the powerful vested interest that will inevitably oppose it.

Notes

1 See for example Righelato and Spracklen (2007).
2 Tulip and Michaels (2004), p. 35.
3 Gran (1982).
4 This is described in detail in Jawara and Kwa (2004). The book contains descriptions of the bullying techniques used, with examples.

Bibliography

ActionAid International (2005) 'Power Hungry: Six Reasons to Regulate Global Food Corporations', www.actionaid.org/main.aspx?PageID=202 (November 2007).

ADB (Asian Development Bank) (2007) 'Purchasing Power Parity: Preliminary Report', 2005 International Comparison Program in Asia and the Pacific, Manila, www.adb.org/Documents/Reports/ICP-Purchasing-Power-Parity/Main-Report.pdf (November 2007).

Addison of Stallingborough, Lord (1939) *A Policy for British Agriculture*, Victor Gollancz, London.

AERC (African Economic Research Consortium) (2007) 'Managing Commodity Booms in Sub-Saharan Africa', *Policy Brief* No. 2, June, Nairobi, www.aercafrica.org/documents/policybriefs/policy_ brief_2.pdf (November 2007).

Agritrade (2007) 'Coffee: Executive brief', Technical Centre for Agricultural and Rural Cooperation ACP-EU, Wageningen, Netherlands, agritrade.cta.int/en/commodities/coffee_sector/executive_brief (August 2007).

Alam, M. S. (2006) 'Global Disparities since 1800: Trends and Regional Patterns', *Journal of World-Systems Research* 12 (2): 37–59, jwsr.ucr.edu/archive/vol12/number1/pdf/jwsr-v12n1-alam.pdf and mpra.ub.uni-muenchen. de/1289 (October 2007).

Ashley, C. and S. Maxwell (2001) 'Rethinking Rural Development', *Development Policy Review* 19 (4) (December).

Bagchi, A. K. (1982) *The Political Economy of Underdevelopment*, Cambridge University Press, Cambridge.

Bairoch, P. (1992) *Economic and World History*, Wheatsheaf, Brighton.

Banana Link (2005) *Banana Trade News Bulletin* 33, Norwich, UK, www.bananalink.org.uk/index.php?option=com_content&task=view&id=100 (November 2007).

—— (2007) *Banana Trade News Bulletin* 38, Norwich, UK, www.bananalink.org.uk/index.php?option=com_content&task=view&id=100 (November 2007).

Berkman, S. (2007) 'The World Bank and the $100 Billion Question' in S. Hiatt (ed.), *A Game as Old as Empire: the Secret World of Economic Hit Men and the Web of Global Corruption*, Berrett-Koehler, San Francisco.

Blas, J. (2007) 'Wheat Prices Jump to Record High', *Financial Times*, 24 August, www.ft.com/cms/s/0/9939d268-51b8-11dc-8779-0000779fd2ac.html (September 2007).

Bridger, R. (2007) 'The Chill-Chain in the Sky', unpublished; this is an extended version of 'The Chill-Chain in the Sky: Aviation's Fastest Growing Sector', in proceedings of Green Economics Conference, Oxford, April 2007, available on request via www.greeneconomics. org.uk/page212.html (November 2007).

Brown, O., A. Crawford and J. Gibson (2008) 'Boom or Bust: How Commodity Price Volatility Impedes Poverty Reduction, and What to Do About It', published by the International Institute for Sustainable Development, Winnipeg, Canada, www.iisd.org./pdf/2008/boom-or-bust-commodity.pdf (April 2008).

Brown, O. and C. Sander (2007) 'Supermarket Buying Power: Global Supply Chains and Smallholder Farmers', International Institute for Sustainable Development, Winnipeg, Canada, www.tradeknowledgenetwork.net (November 2007).

Buckman, G. (2005) *Global Trade: Past Mistakes, Future Choices*, Zed Books, London.

Buncombe, A. (2007) 'Indian Shopkeepers Force New Supermarkets to Close', *The Independent*, 27 August, London, news.independent.co.uk/world/asia/article2898433.ece (October 2007).

Business America (1985), 28 October, findarticles.com/p/articles/mi_m1052/is_v8/ai_3993311 (February 2008).

Business Times (Malaysia) (2005) 25 July.

Butler, R. A. (2005) 'Collapsing Vanilla Prices Will Affect Madagascar', on mongabay.com, 9 May, news.mongabay.com/2005/0510-rhett_butler. html (August 2005).

Chang, H.-J. (2007) 'Protectionism: The Truth Is on a $10 Bill', *The Independent*, 23 July, London, news.independent.co.uk/business/comment/article 2793124.ece (November 2007).

Chomsky, N. (1993) *Year 501: The Conquest Continues*, www.zmag.org/Chomsky/year/year-overview.html (June 2007).

Christian Aid (2005) 'Business as Usual: the World Bank, the IMF and the Liberalisation Agenda', London.

Collier, P. (2007) *The Bottom Billion: Why the Poorest Countries Are Failing and What Can Be Done about It*, Oxford University Press, Oxford and New York.

COMESA (Common Market for Eastern and Southern Africa) and Michigan State University (undated) 'Enhancing African Food Security through Improved Regional Marketing Systems for Food Staples', www.aec.msu.edu/ fs2/ outreach/comesa-msu_policy_research_ agenda.pdf (November 2007).

Conway, G. (1997) *The Doubly Green Revolution*, Penguin, Harmondsworth.

Daviron, B. and S. Ponte (2005) *The Coffee Paradox: Global Markets, Commodity Trade and the Elusive Promise of Development*, Zed Books, London and New York.

DEFRA (Department for the Environment, Food and Rural Affairs) (2007a) 'Price Indices for Products and Inputs', March 29, London, statistics. defra.gov.uk/esg/publications/auk/2006/table4-1.xls (November 2007).

——— (2007b) 'Changes in Retail Price Indices', March 29, London,statistics. defra.gov.uk/esg/publications/auk/2006/chart7-8.xls (November 2007).

Dembele, D. M. (2004) 'The International Monetary Fund and World Bank in Africa', *Pambazuka News*, 24 September, www.pambazuka.org/index. php?issue=175 (September 2007).

Deutscher Welthungerhilfe, IFPRI and Concern Worldwide (2007) *The Challenge of Hunger 2007*, Bonn, www.ifpri.org/media/20071012ghi/ghi07.pdf (October 2007).

Diao, X., P. Dorosh and S. M. Rahman (2003) 'Market Opportunities for African Agriculture: an Examination of Demand-Side Constraints on Agricultural Growth', DSGD Discussion Paper No. 1, International Food Policy Research Institute, Washington, www.ifpri.org/divs/dsgd/dp/dsgdp01.htm (November 2007).

Diao, X., P. Hazell, D. Resnick and J. Thurlow (2007) 'The Role of Agriculture in Development: Implications for Sub-Saharan Africa', Research Report No. 153, International Food Policy Research Institute, Washington, www.ifpri.org/pubs/abstract/rr153.asp (November 2007).

EcoNews Africa (2005) 'EPAs – Threats to Development in Africa: Statement by EcoNews Africa', 23 June, Nairobi.

FAO, Food and Agriculture Organization (2004a) *The State of Agricultural Commodity Markets 2004*, Rome, www.fao.org/docrep/007/y5419e/y5419e00.htm (November 2007).

―― (2004b) *The State of Food Insecurity in the World 2004*, Rome, www.fao.org/docrep/007/y5650e/y5650e00.htm (November 2007).

―― (2005) *Small Island Developing States: Agricultural Production and Trade, Preferences and Policy*, FAO Commodities and Trade Technical Paper No. 7, Rome www.fao.org/docrep/007/y5795e/y5795e00.htm (November 2007).

―― (2006) *The State of Food Insecurity in the World 2006*, Rome, www.fao.org/docrep/009/a0750e/a0750e00.htm (November 2007).

―― (2007) *Food Outlook: Global Market Analysis*, June, Rome, www.fao.org/giews/english/fo/index.htm (November 2007).

FEWS NET (Famine Early Warning Systems Network) (2007a) *Djibouti: Food Security Update*, October, www.fews.net/centers/innerSections.aspx?f=dj&pageID=monthliesDoc&m=1002602 (November 2007).

―― (2007b) *Informal Cross Border Food Trade in Southern Africa* 34 (July–August), www.fews.net/special/index.aspx?pageID=genericDoc&g=1001441 (November 2007).

FNSEA (Fédération Nationale des Syndicats d'Exploitants Agricoles) (2007) 'A Structural Imbalance in the Balance of Power', www.copa-cogeca.be/pdf/ip122x2e.pdf (September 2007).

Gaidar, Y. (2007) 'The Soviet Collapse: Grain and oil', *On the Issues*, April 19, American Enterprise Institute for Public Policy Research, Washington, www.aei.org/publications/pubID.25991,filter.all/pub_detail.asp (October 2007).

Gale, F. (ed.) (2002) 'China's Food and Agriculture: Issues for the 21st Century', *Agriculture Information Bulletin* No. 775, Economic Research Service, United States Department of Agriculture, Washington, www.ers.usda.gov/publications/ aib775 (August 2007).

Ghosh, J. (2004) 'India Shining, India Declining', International Development Economics Associates, www.ideaswebsite.org/themes/political/feb2004/po05_India_Shining.htm (September 2007).

Gibbon, P. (2007) 'Agro-Commodity Dependence and Recent Trends in Agro-Commodity Markets', DIIS Working Paper 2007/19, Danish Institute for International Studies, Copenhagen, www.dcism.dk/sw42320.asp (November 2007).

Godinot, X. *et al.* (2005) 'Contribution to the Moving out of Poverty Study:

Family Monographs from Burkina Faso and Peru', presented at the World Bank's Annual Bank Conference on Development Economics, Amsterdam, www.siteresources.worldbank.org/INTAMSTERDAM/Resources/Godinot Handout.pdf (November 2007).

Goswami, B. (2007) 'Can Indian Dairy Cooperatives Survive in the New Economic Order?', presented at WTO Public Forum 2007, Geneva, www.wto.org/english/forums_e/public_forum2007_e/session11_goswami _e.pdf (November 2007).

Graffham, A. (2007) 'Public and Private Standards: Trends in the Horticulture Export Sector from Sub-Saharan Africa', *Regoverning Markets* programme, www.regoverningmarkets.org/en/filemanager/active?fid=505 (September 2007).

Graffham, A. and J. MacGregor (2006) 'Impact of EurepGAP on Small-scale Vegetable Growers in Zambia', *Fresh Insights* No. 5 (September), International Institute for Environment and Development, London, www.agrifoodstandards.net/en/filemanager/active?fid=82 (September 2007).

Gran, G. (1982) 'Reviews', *The Multinational Monitor* 3 (2) (February), www.multinationalmonitor.org/hyper/issues/1982/02/reviews.html (September 2007).

Guillaumont, P. (2005) 'Macro Vulnerability in Low Income Countries and Aid Responses', presented at the World Bank's Annual Bank Conference on Development Economics, Amsterdam, siteresources.worldbank.org/ INTAMSTERDAM/Resources/PatrickGuillaumont.pdf (November 2007).

Gupta, B. (2004) 'The History of the International Tea Market, 1850–1945' in EH.Net Encyclopedia, www.eh.net/encyclopedia/article/gupta.tea (April 2006).

Hall, J. (2007) 'Suppliers Suffer from Supermarket Price Cuts', *Sunday Telegraph*, London, 26 August, www.telegraph.co.uk/news/main.jhtml?xml=/ news/2007/08/26/nrfood126.xml (September 2007).

Hightower, J. (1973) 'Food, Farmers, Corporations, Earl Butz ... and You', mimeo, Agribusiness Accountability Project, Washington.

Hossain, M. (1990) 'Bangladesh: Economic Performance and Prospects', ODI Briefing Paper, ODI, London.

Humphrey, J. (2000) 'Pressures on Companies to Comply with Standards: Do They Open up or Close off Market Access for Developing Countries Suppliers?', presentation made at ODI, London.

IFAD (International Fund for Agricultural Development) (2001) *Rural Poverty Report 2001: The Challenge of Ending Rural Poverty*, Rome, www.ifad.org/ poverty/ index.htm (August 2005).

Ihiga, S. (2005) 'Assessment of Kenya's Export Potential to EU for Non-Agricultural Products', research study for Keplotrade.

Imber, V., J. Morrison and A. Thomson (2003) *Food Security, Trade and Livelihoods Linkages*, Oxford Policy Management, Oxford, and Department for International Development, London.

IMF (International Monetary Fund) (2005) 'Dealing with the Revenue Consequences of Trade Reform', Washington, www.imf.org/external/ np/pp/eng/2005/021505.pdf (July 2007).

Independent Evaluation Group (2007) 'World Bank Assistance to Agriculture in

Sub-Saharan Africa: an IEG Review', Washington, World Bank, siteresources.worldbank.org/EXTASSAGRSUBSAHAFR/Resources/ag_africa_ev al.pdf (February 2008).

IRIN (Integrated Regional Information Networks) (2005) 'Madagascar: Vanilla Farmers Struggle as Prices Plummet', 4 August, www.irinnews.org/Report. aspx?ReportId=55709 (September 2007), reprinted in www.alertnet.org (September 2007).

Issa, O. (2005) 'Labour-Niger: Gold Miners Exploit Children', Inter Press Service News Agency, 26 August, www.ipsnews.net/news.asp?idnews= 30037 (August 2005).

Jasny, N. (1951) 'Kolkhozy, the Achilles Heel of the Soviet Regime', *Soviet Studies* 3 (2) (October): 150–63.

Jawara, F., and A. Kwa (2004) (updated edition) *Behind the Scenes at the WTO: the Real World of International Trade Negotiations*, London and New York, Zed Books.

Kanji, N., C. Vijfhuizen, C. Braga and L. Artur (2004), 'Trade Liberalisation, Gender and Livelihoods: the Mozambican Cashew Nut Case', prepared for the Eleventh World Congress of Rural Sociology, Trondheim, Norway.

Kaplinsky, R. (2005) *Globalization, Poverty and Inequality: Between a Rock and a Hard Place*, Polity Press, Cambridge.

Keidel, A. (2007) 'The Limits of a Smaller, Poorer China', *Financial Times*, 14 November, London, www.ft.com/cms/s/0/4eaba8b0-9255-11dc-8981-0000779fd2 ac.html (November 2007).

Keynes, J. M. (1946) [1980] 'The International Control of Raw Material Prices' in *The Collected Writings of John Maynard Keynes*, Vol. 27, Macmillan, London.

Kydd, J., A. Dorward, J. Morrison and G. Cadisch (2002) 'Agricultural Development and Pro Poor Economic Growth in Sub Saharan Africa: Potential and Policy', ADU Working Paper No. 02/04, Imperial College, Wye, Ashford.

Lapper, R. (2007) 'Globalisation's Exiles Keep the Home Fires Burning', *Financial Times*, 28 August.

Leith, J. C. (2005) *Why Botswana Prospered*, McGill-Queen's University Press, Montreal.

Lines, T. (1989) 'In Praise of Cartels: Oligopoly Effects in the Aluminium Industry', presented at European International Business Association Conference, Helsinki.

—— (1990) 'Restructuring of the Aluminium Industry: Implications for Developing Countries', *Development Policy Review* 8 (3).

—— (2004) 'Commodities Trade, Poverty Alleviation and Sustainable Development: the Re-emerging Debate', Common Fund for Commodities, Amsterdam, www.tomlines.org.uk (November 2007).

—— (2006) 'Market Power, Price Determination and Primary Commodities', TRADE Research Paper No. 10, South Centre, Geneva, www.southcentre. org/publications/researchpapers/ResearchPapers10.pdf and www.tomlines. org.uk (November 2007).

Lucas, R. E. (2004) 'The Industrial Revolution: Past and Future' in *The Region*, 2003 Annual Report issue, Federal Reserve Bank of Minneapolis, www.minneapolisfed.org/pubs/region/04-05/essay.cfm (May 2007).

Lynn, B. C. (2006) 'The Case for Breaking up Wal-Mart', in *Harper's*, www.alternet.org/story/39251 (September 2007).

MacBean, A. I. and D. T. Nguyen (1987) *Commodity Policies: Problems and Prospects*, Croom Helm, London and Sydney.

Maddison, A. (2001) *The World Economy: a Millennial Perspective*, Organization for Economic Cooperation and Development, Paris.

Maizels, A. (1973) 'UNCTAD and the Commodity Problems of Developing Countries', *IDS Bulletin* 5 (1) (January).

Matin, I. (2005) 'Addressing Vulnerability of the Poorest: a Micro Perspective Based on Brac's Experiences', presented at the World Bank's Annual Bank Conference on Development Economics, Amsterdam, siteresources. world bank.org/INTAMSTERDAM/Resources/ImranMatin.pdf (November 2007).

Maussion, C. (2007) 'La Potion Ultralibérale de la Commission Attali', *Libération*, Paris, 13 October, www.liberation.fr/actualite/economie_terre/284388. FR.php (November 2007).

Murphy, S. (2006) 'Concentrated Market Power and Agricultural Trade', Ecofair Trade Dialogue: Discussion Paper No. 1, Heinrich Böll Foundation, Berlin, www.tradeobservatory.org/library.cfm?refID= 89014 (September 2007).

NACLA (North American Congress on Latin America) (1975) 'US Grain Arsenal', *Latin America and Empire Report* 9 (7) (October), archive.nacla.org/ archive/digitalarchive.aspx?panes=1&aid= 00907001_1 (November 2007).

National Farmers Union (2005) 'The Farm Crisis: Its Causes and Solutions', Kananaskis, Alberta, www.nfu.ca/briefs.html#policy (June 2007).

National Statistics (2006) 'Net Farm Income and Cash Income by Types of Farm in England', statistics.defra.gov.uk/esg/statnot/Octpressrel.pdf (June 2007).

New Vision (Kampala) (2005) 'Vanilla Farmers to Blame for Low Prices', 20 August, allafrica.com/stories/200508220185.html (August 2005).

Nissanke, M. and E. Thorbecke (2007) 'Linking Globalization to Poverty', *South Bulletin* No. 145, 15 May, South Centre, Geneva, www.southcentre.org/info/ southbulletin/bulletin145.pdf (November 2007).

Nolan, P. (1995) *China's Rise, Russia's Fall: Politics, Economics and Planning in the Transition from Stalinism*, Macmillan, London.

Nyapendi, M. (2005) 'Vanilla Price Falls to Sh500 a Kilo', *New Vision* (Kampala), 3 August, allafrica.com/stories/200508030479.html (August 2005).

OAU (Organization of African Unity) (1980) *Lagos Plan of Action for the Economic Development of Africa 1980–2000*, www.uneca.org/itca/ariportal/docs/ lagos_plan.pdf (July 2007).

ODI (Overseas Development Institute) (1988) 'The Rich and the Poor: Changes in Incomes of Developing Countries since 1960,' *ODI Briefing Paper*, London.

Open Door Web Site (2007) 'The "Scramble for Africa"', www.saburchill.com/ history/chapters/empires/0056.html (March 2008).

Oxfam International (2002) 'Mugged: Poverty in Your Coffee Cup', www.oxfam.org.uk/resources/papers/downloades/mugged.pdf/ (April 2008), Oxford.

—— (2004) 'Trading away Our Rights: Women Working in Global Supply Chains', Oxfam Campaign Report, Oxford, www.oxfam.org/en/policy/ briefingnotes/report_042008_labor (November 2007).

Patnaik, U. (2004) 'The Republic of Hunger', public lecture given in New Delhi, www.ideaswebsite.org/themes/agriculture/apr2004/ag21_Republic_ Hunger.htm (October 2007).

Paul, N. C. (2003) 'Vanilla Sky High', *The Christian Science Monitor*, 11 August, www.csmonitor.com/2003/0811/p13s02-wmcn.html (August 2005).

Pay, E. (2005) 'Overview of the Sanitary and Phytosanitary Measures in QUAD Countries on Tropical Fruits and Vegetables Imported from Developing Countries', TRADE Research Paper No. 1, South Centre, Geneva, www.southcentre.org/publications/researchpapers/ResearchPapers1.pdf (September 2007).

Pearson, L. B. (1969) *Partners in Development: Report of the Commission on International Development*, Pall Mall Press, London.

PriceWaterhouseCoopers (2005) 'Sustainability Impact Assessment (SIA) of the EU–ACP Economic Partnership Agreements: Phase Two', Paris, trade.ec. europa.eu/doclib/docs/2007/march/tradoc_133936.pdf (November 2007).

Rabobank International (2004) *Rabobank View on Food and Agriculture 2004: Changes in the Global Food System*, Utrecht, Netherlands.

Ravallion, M. and G. Datt (1996) 'How Important to India's Poor Is the Sectoral Composition of Economic Growth?', *The World Bank Economic Review* 10 (1): 1–26.

Reardon, T., C. P. Timmer and J. Berdegue (2003a) 'The Rise of Supermarkets and Private Standards in Developing Countries: Illustrations from the Produce Sector and Hypothesized Implications for Trade', presented at conference on 'Agricultural Policy Reform and the WTO: Where Are We Heading?', Capri, Italy.

Reardon, T., C. P. Timmer, C. B. Barrett and J. Berdegue (2003b) 'The Rise of Supermarkets in Africa, Asia, and Latin America', *American Journal of Agricultural Economics* 85 (5).

Republic of Kenya (2007) 'Brief on COMESA', Nairobi, www.comesasummit. go.ke/docs/BRIEF%20ON%20COMESA%20SUMMIT%20feb2007.pdf (November 2007).

Reuters (2007) report, 6 August, investing.reuters.co.uk/news/articleinvesting. aspx?type=tnBusinessNews&storyID=2007-08-06T091341Z_01_ BOM101853_ RTRIDST_0_BUSINESS-BHARTI-WALMART-DC.XML (August 2007).

Righelato, R. and D. V. Spracklen (2007) 'Carbon Mitigation by Biofuels or by Saving and Restoring Forests?', *Science* 317 (17 August): 902, www.science mag.org/cgi/content/full/317/5840/902 or by request via reporter. leeds.ac.uk/press_releases/current/biofuels.htm (November 2007).

Ross, M. (2001) *Extractive Sectors and the Poor*, Oxfam America, Boston, www.oxfamamerica.org/newsandpublications/publications/research_reports /art2635.html (July 2007).

Rowell, A. and J. Marriott (2007) 'Mercenaries on the Front Lines in the New Scramble for Africa' in S. Hiatt (ed.), *A Game as Old as Empire: the Secret World of Economic Hit Men and the Web of Global Corruption*, Berrett-Koehler, San Francisco.

Russell, A. (2007) 'Angola Forces China to Rethink Its Approach', *Financial Times*, 24 August, London.

Santiso, J. (2005) 'Angel or Devil? Chinese Trade Impact on Latin American Emerging Markets', presented at the World Bank's Annual Bank Conference on Development Economics, Amsterdam, siteresources.worldbank.org/ INTAMSTERDAM/Resources/JavierSantisoPaper.pdf (November 2007).

Schiff, M. (1995) 'Commodity Exports and the Adding-up Problem in LDCs: Trade, Investment and Lending Policy', *World Development* 23 (4).

Sender, J. (2002) 'The Struggle to Escape Poverty in South Africa: Results from a Purposive Survey', *Journal of Agrarian Change* 2 (1): 1–49.

Sender, J. (2003) 'Rural Poverty and Gender: Analytical Frameworks and Policy Proposals' in H.-J. Chang (ed.), *Rethinking Development Economics*, Anthem Press, London.

Sguazzin, A. (2005) 'Impala to Study $2.25 Billion Madagascar Nickel Plan', 26 May, Bloomberg.com, www.bloomberg.com/apps/news?pid=10000082&sid=a54BnWQuaF5g&refer=canada (November 2007).

Shafaeddin, M. (2006) 'Does Trade Openness Favour or Hinder Industrialization and Development?', TWN Trade and Development Series No. 31, Third World Network, Penang, Malaysia, available at www.twnside. org.sg/title/tnd/td31.htm (November 2007).

Smith, A. (1982) *The Wealth of Nations: Books I–III*, Penguin English Library, London.

Solimano, A. (2001) 'The Evolution of World Income Inequality: Assessing the Impact of Globalization', UN Economic Commission for Latin America and the Caribbean, Santiago, Chile, www.eclac.org/de/publicaciones/xml/0/ 9220/lcl1686i.pdf (October 2007).

Stein, H. (2003) 'Rethinking African Development' in H.-J. Chang (ed.), *Rethinking Development Economics*, Anthem Press, London.

Tan, C. (2005) 'Evolving Aid Modalities and Their Impact on the Delivery of Essential Services in Low-Income Countries', *Law, Social Justice and Global Development Journal* 1, www.go.warwick.ac.uk/elj/lgd/2005_1/tan (July 2007).

The Economist (2005) 'The Harnessing of Nature's Bounty', 5 November.

The Hindu Business Line (2006) 3 April, www.thehindubusinessline.com/2006/04/03/stories/2006040301030500.htm (July 2007).

The Telegraph (Kolkata) (2006) 6 March.

Traidcraft (2005) 'Are International Supply Chains Increasing Poverty?', London.

Tulip, K., and L. Michaels (2004) 'A Rough Guide to the UK Farming Crisis', Corporate Watch, Oxford, www.corporatewatch.org.uk/download .php?id=46 (November 2007).

UNCTAD (UN Conference on Trade and Development) (2002) *The Least Developed Countries Report 2002: Escaping the Poverty Trap*, New York and Geneva, www.unctad.org/Templates/Page.asp?intItemID=3073&lang=1 (November 2007).

—— (2003a) *Commodity Yearbook 1995–2000, Vol. II*, Geneva.

—— (2003b) *Economic Development in Africa: Trade Performance and Commodity Dependence*, New York and Geneva, www.unctad.org/Templates/webflyer. asp?docid=4375&intItemID=1528&lang=1 (February 2006).

—— (2003c) 'Market Access, Market Entry and Competitiveness', document no. TD/B/COM.1/65, Geneva, www.unctad.org/en/docs/c1d65_en.pdf (August 2007).

—— (2003d) 'Report of the Meeting of Eminent Persons on Commodity Issues Held at the Palais des Nations, Geneva, 22–23 September 2003', Geneva, r0.unctad.org/commodities/docs/tb50d11_en.pdf (August 2007).

—— (2004) *The Least Developed Countries Report 2004: Linking International Trade with Poverty Reduction*, New York and Geneva.

—— (2005) *Statistical Profiles of the Least Developed Countries*, United Nations, New York and Geneva, www.unctad.org/Templates/Page.asp?int ItemID=3641&lang=1 (November 2007).

—— (2006a) *The Least Developed Countries Report 2006: Developing Productive Capacities*, New York and Geneva, www.unctad.org/Templates/Page.asp?int ItemID=3073&lang=1 (November 2007).

—— (2006b) *Trade and Development Report, 2006: Global Partnership and National Policies for Development*, New York and Geneva, www.unctad.org/Templates/WebFlyer.asp?intItemID=3921&lang=1 (October 2007).

—— (2007) 'Food Safety and Environmental Requirements in Export Markets – Friend or Foe for Producers of Fruit and Vegetables in Asian Developing Countries?', document no. UNCTAD/DITC/TED/2006/8, Geneva, www.unctad.org/en/docs/ ditcted20068_en.pdf (September 2007).

UNCTAD (UN Conference on Trade and Development) and Common Fund for Commodities (2004) *Commodity Atlas*, New York and Geneva, www.unctad.org/en/docs/ditccom20041fas_en.pdf (November 2007).

UNDP (UN Development Programme) (1999) *Human Development Report 1999*, Oxford University Press, New York and Oxford, hdr.undp.org/ reports/global/1999/en/ (July 2007).

—— (2003) *Human Development Report 2003: Millennium Development Goals: A Compact among Nations to End Human Poverty*, Oxford University Press, New York and Oxford, hdr.undp.org/xmlsearch/reportSearch?y=*&c=g&t=*&k= (November 2007).

—— (2004) *Human Development Report 2004: Cultural Liberty in Today's Diverse World*, Oxford University Press, New York and Oxford, hdr.undp.org/xmlsearch/reportSearch?y=*&c=g&t=*&k= (November 2007).

—— (2005) *Human Development Report 2005: International Cooperation at a Crossroads: Aid, Trade and Security in an Unequal World*, Oxford University Press, New York and Oxford, hdr.undp.org/xmlsearch/reportSearch?y=*&c=g&t=*&k= (November 2007).

—— (2006) *Human Development Report 2006: Beyond Scarcity: Power, Poverty and the Global Water Crisis*, Oxford University Press, New York and Oxford, hdr.undp.org/xmlsearch/reportSearch?y=*&c=g&t=*&k= (November 2007).

van de Kasteele, A. and M. van der Stichele (2005) 'Update on the Banana Chain' in European Banana Action Network *et al.*, *International Banana Conference II: Reversing the 'Race to the Bottom:' Preparatory Papers*, Brussels, www.ibc2.org/images/stories/textibc/finadoc.pdf (November 2007).

Vander Stichele, M., S. van der Waal and J. Oldenziel (2006) *Who Reaps the Fruit? Critical Issues in the Fresh Fruit and Vegetable Chain*, SOMO, Amsterdam, www.somo.nl/html/paginas/pdf/Who_reaps_the_fruit_june_2006_EN.pdf (November 2006).

Volkogonov, D. (1995) *Lenin: Life and Legacy*, translated by Harold Shukman, London, Harper Collins.

Vorley, B. (2003) *Food, Inc.: Corporate Concentration from Farm to Consumer*, UK Food Group, London, www.ukfg.org.uk/docs/UKFG-Foodinc-Nov03.pdf (September 2007).

Vorley, B. and T. Fox (2004a) 'Concentration in Food Supply and Retail Chains', Working Paper No. 13, Department for International Development, London, dfid-agriculture-consultation.nri.org/summaries/wp13.pdf (August 2007).

—— (2004b) 'Global Food Chains: Constraints and Opportunities for Small-holders', presented at the Agriculture and Pro-poor Growth Task Team Workshop, Helsinki.

Wade, R. H. (2005) 'What Strategies are Viable for Developing Countries Today? The World Trade Organization and the Shrinking of "Development Space"', in K. P. Gallagher (ed.), *Putting Development First: the Importance of Policy Space in the WTO and IFIs*, Zed Books, London and New York, pp. 80–101.

Wallis, W. (2007) 'Oil Find Raises Stakes on Congo Border', Special Report on Uganda, *Financial Times*, 20 November.

White House (2001) 'President's Remarks to the Future Farmers of America', 27 July, Washington, www.whitehouse.gov/news/releases/2001/07/ 20010727-2.html (February 2008).

World Bank (1981) *Accelerated Development in Sub-Saharan Africa: an Agenda for Action*. World Bank, Washington DC.

—— (1986) *World Development Report 1986*, New York, Oxford University Press.

—— (1996) *Global Economic Prospects and the Developing Countries*, World Bank, Washington DC.

—— (2001) *World Development Report 2000/2001: Attacking Poverty*, Oxford University Press, New York.

WTO (World Trade Organization) (2006) 'Modalities for Negotiations on Agricultural Commodity Issues: Proposal Submitted by the African Group to the Special Session of the Committee on Agriculture', document no. TN/AG/GEN/18, Geneva, www.wto.org/english/forums_e/public_ forum_e/comm_position_afr_group_june706.pdf (November 2007).

Yee, A. (2007) 'Engaging India: a Matter of National Shame', *Financial Times*, 23 August.

Index

A&P (Great Atlantic and Pacific Tea Company), 114-15
'accelerated development', policies, 123
Afghanistan, poppies, 44
Africa, 3, 24, 58, 127; aid programmes, 36; cattle importance, 128; cocoa producers, 63; colonial formations, 30, 33, 129; crops, 132; domestic market importance, 125; food imports, 120; independence outcomes, 34; land-locked countries, 18; mining industry decline, 46-7; national fragmentation, 134; poverty concentration, 16; regional trade, 130-1, 147; stagnation experience, 2; staple foods, 124; sub-Saharan, *see* sub-Saharan Africa; super-market investment, 95; terms of trade, 21; total population, 17; vegetable export promotion, 80; world coffee export share, 48
African Economic Community, project of, 36
African Union, 136
agribusiness, geographical concentration, 98
agriculture: British, 145; commodities price vulnerability, 20-1; crop unpre-dictability, 67; domestic prices undercut, 46; exports, 48; national marketing boards, 55, 95, 130; 1990s crisis, 24; profitability undermined, 22; women's manual labour, 8; *see also*, farming; food
airfreight, 96, 105; fish, 82
Albania, remittances importance, 65
aluminium, price controls, 84
Angola, 20, 62, 143; Chinese investment in, 47; oil export dependence, 21
animal welfare, 109
Aral Sea, drying up, 19

Argentina, 34, 140; ISA policy, 37; soya monoculture, 103
Asian Development Bank, 24
Association of South-East Asian Nations (ASEAN), 134
AT&T, break-up, 111

bananas, 65, 72, 78, 94, 124, 130, 143; cheap offer pressures, 104; East Africa, 132; EU quotas, 76, 123; export regulated, 85; exporting countries, 77; TNCs, 99
Bangladesh, 134-5; *per capita* growth rate, 18; poverty, 8; sugar price, 78
Barbados, 78
beef, EU quotas, 76
Belgium, 98
Bengal, colonial impoverishment, 32, 34, 49
Benin, cotton, 64
Berg, Elliot, World Bank Report, 35-7, 50, 55, 57, 83, 130, 148
Bharatiya Janata Party, India (BJP), 24
Bharti Enterprises, 95
biofuels, 79, 143; maize demand, 63
Bolivia, 18, 143
Botswana, 128, 130; diamond exports, 145; state economic planning, 54-5
Brazil, 24, 34, 98, 125; agricultural exports, 131; coffee, 48; farm size, 101-2; ISI policy, 37; soya monocul-ture, 103
Brezhnev, L., 120
Britain: colonialism, 31-2, 140; Industrial Revolution, 3; Opium Wars, 34; pro-tectionism, 53; *see also*, United Kingdom
buffer stocks, 86-8
Bukhara, 19
Bunge, 93

Burkina Faso: cotton, 64; education lack, 23
Burundi, 77; malnutrition, 123
Bush, George W., 118, 123-4, 128
'bushmeat', recourse to, 82
buyer power: corporate, 80, 96; supply chains, 112

Cadbury Schweppes, profit margins, 97
Canada: farm incomes, 23; supply management, 83
Cargill, 93
Carrefour, supermarket chain, 102
cassava, 9, 120, 124, 130, 132; African production, 125; varieties, 126; World Bank negativity to, 127
Chad, cotton, 64
Chaudhuri, K.N., 31
child labour campaigns, 109
Chile, copper mining, 47
China, 15, 18, 22, 30, 123, 130, 147; Africa investments, 47, 143; agricultural de-collectivization, 44; atypicality, 5; authoritarian character, 51; British Opium Wars, 34; economic progress, 50; EPZs, 79; food exports, 120; food self-sufficiency policy, 101, 119, 146; income inequality, 24; industrial development, 135-6; infrastructure, 131; population, 17; raw material imports, 61, 64; rural, 25, 148; supermarkets, 95; tea, 85
Chiquita, 99
climate change, 19, 26
cloves, 90
Côte d'Ivoire, 126
cocoa, 33, 72, 76, 78, 85, 87; global price fall, 41, 63; oversupply, 71
coffee, 72, 90, 118, 143; Association of Coffee Producing Countries, 89; British market, 73; corporate concentration, 97-8; Ethiopia, 69-70; export quotas, 77-8, 91; fairtrade movement's floor price, 65; global export shares, 48; International Coffee Agreement, 83, 87-8; oversupply, 71; price cycles, 76; roaster corporations, 94, 99, 102; world price volatility, 41, 49, 63, 76
'cold chain', food, 79
Colombia: coca, 44; coffee, 48, 102; flower exports, 73
commodities: compensatory finance, 70;

financial derivatives, 67-8; horticultural, 81; non-traditional, 79-80, 106; marketing boards, 39; oversupply, 71; price volatility, 20-1, 41, 62-3, 66, 69, 76; 'supercycle', 61
Common Market for Eastern and Southern Africa (COMESA), 130, 135
comparative advantage, theory of, 39, 118, 133
competition: anti-trust laws, 111; idea of global authority, 113; policy inadequacy, 112
consumer campaigns, 102
Cool Chain Association, 79
cooperatives, dairy, 127
copper, 33, 65, 90; Chilean export dominance, 47; futures exchanges, 69; price rise, 62
corporate power, concentrations of, 80, 96, 138
Costa Rica, plantation wages, 99
cotton, 65, 76, 118; EU subsidies, 78; real price fall, 63; slave economy, 30-1; subsidies, 72; US subsidies, 64
country income categories, 9
Czech Republic, 78

Danone, 114
De Beers, 84, 145
Del Monte, 99
delivery schedules, fresh produce, 105
demand elasticity/inelasticity, 41, 67, 72
Dembele, D.M., 57
Democratic Republic (DR) of Congo, 48; copper mining, 33, 47; malnutrition, 123; personal income collapse, 15
Deng Hsiao-ping, 53
'dependency theory', 34
'developmental state', planning requirement, 53
Dhaka, 32
diamonds: Central Selling Organization, 145; controlled world market, 55, 84
diversification, reduction of, 49
Djibouti, 146; food import dependency, 123
Dole, 99
dollar US, value fall, 41
domestic markets, development need, 133
Douwe-Egberts, 97

East Asia, countries of, 18

East India Company (EIC), 30-2; trade pattern, 6
East Timor, *per capita* incomes, 16
economies of scale, 17, 19, 24, 100-1, 147; retail, 97
Ecuador, 143; banana export regulated, 85
education, 23; standards of, 14
Eritrea, 21
Ethiopia, 77; air transport business, 21; chat, 44; coffee, 69-71, 102; malnutrition, 123
Europe, imperialism, 140
European Economic Community (EEC), 135, 142; Common Agricultural Policy, 86
European Union, 134, 135; ACP Sugar Protocol, 77; bananas, 123; cotton subsidies, 64, 72; Commission, 71, 111; Economic Partnership Agreements, 136; food standards, 106; import quotas, 77; Lomé agreements Stabex, 70; market preferential access, 76; quota guarantees, 55; sugar quotas, 145
export orientation, model, 36, 38, 46, 71, 144; colonial pattern, 44; costs of, 43; dogma, 62, 148; *see also*, fallacy of composition
export processing zones, coastal, 79, 144
export revenue, 21, 39
exports, commodities, 15; internationally managed, 55; privileged, 147; volume-price gap, 62
ExxonMobil, 115

fairtrade campaigns, 109
'fallacy of composition', export-led growth, 39, 42, 72, 80; cocoa, 63
farming: British, 23-4, 73; corporate input control, 94; detailed requirements of, 106; environmental consequences, 102, 128; monocultural, 102-3; operating size, 101; risk transferred to, 93, 103-105; *see also*, agriculture; food
Fiji, EU sugar quota, 78
fish, 76; airfreighted, 82
flowers, British supermarkets, 73
food: airfreight infrastructure, 79; corporate geography, 98; inelastic demand, 67; 'normal' standards perceptions, 16; processing companies, 97; production land loss, 44; regional

trade, 131; retail concentration, 95; safety, 106; security, national/regional, 53, 118-19, 146-7; standards imposition, 107; vertical integration, 94
Food and Agriculture Organization of the UN (FAO), 95, 101, 120, 125, 132; low income food-deficit countries category, 22
Ford, Gerald, 119, 123
foreign aid, 20; exports priority, 45
foreign debt, write-offs, 56
France, 113
fruit juices, 76
futures exchange, commodities, 69

GATT (General Agreement on Tariffs and Trade), 45, 106; Uruguay Round, 142
Germany, 20; industrialization protectionism, 53
Ghana, 19, 33; food imports, 126; gold production revival, 47; vegetable imports, 82
Global Cassava Development Strategy, (GCDS), 125-7
GlobalGAP (ex-EurepGAP), 108-9
Godinot, Xavier, 8
gold, 33
'good governance': agenda of, 56; rhetoric, 50-2
Gorbachev, Mikhail, 119
grain, intra-Africa, 131
Gran, Guy, 57, 148
Great Depression, 141
Group of 90, WTO, 85
Guatemala, coffee, 102
Guyana, EU sugar quota, 78

Haiti, remittances importance, 65
hedging, theory of, 69
Highly Indebted Poor Countries (HIPC) initiative, 56
HIV/Aids, 26
Homegrown Ltd, 100
Hong Kong, migrant labour, 65
horticulture, ad hoc contracts, 105; commodities, 81; Kenya, 100; water use, 80
Houphouët-Boigny, Félix, 126
Hudson Bay Company, 30
human development, 'low' definition, 15
Human Development Index (HDI), 14, 16

Hungary, 78
hunger: definitions, 7; smallholder farming communities, 6

ILO (International Labour Organization): employment laws, 110; labour standards, 146
IMF (International Monetary Fund), 35, 57-8, 71, 142-3; Compensatory Finance Facility, 70; conditionality, 89; creation, 141; economic stabilization programmes, 37; financial crisis, 56; 'good governance' ideology, 50, Madagascar interference, 42; stabilization programmes, 46; structural adjustment policies, *see* structural adjustment; Special Drawing Rights, 41
imports: duties, 46; quotas, 85; substitution policies, 37; variety requirement, 45
India, 15, 18, 22, 30, 123, 130, 140, 147; atypicality, 5; British rule, 33; cashew nut market, 50; child malnourishment, 25; EIC trade pattern, 44; emigrant labour, 65; food self-sufficiency aim, 53, 119, 146; income inequality, 24; industrial development, 136; milk production, 127; Mutiny 1857, 31; population, 17; rural poverty, 148; supermarket rarity, 95; tea, 85; Tesco lobbying, 112; textiles economy, 32; vanilla growing, 42
Indonesia, 30, 91; price stabilization plan, 85; threat to wildlife, 102; vanilla, 78
Industrial Revolution, 3
inequality, 2-3, 14, 24
infrastructure: import requirements, 45; China, 131; *see also*, transport
'intellectual property', 14
Inter-American coffee agreement 1940, 84
Interbrew AmBev, 98
internal market sizes, 17
International Coffee Agreement, abandoned, 63
International Commodity Agreements (ICAs), 84, 87, 90
international debt crisis, 1980s, 37, 142, 148
International Food Policy Research Institute (IFPRI), 124, 129, 131
International Fund for Agricultural Development (IFAD), 6-7, 125, 129

International Tea Agreement, 1933, 83
International Tin Agreement, 87, 89-90, abandoned, 64
International Wheat Agreement, 87
Iran (Persia), 34, 64, 1979 revolution, 64
iron ore, price rise, 64

Jacobs, coffe roasters, 97
Jamaica: EU sugar quota, 78; remittances importance, 65
Jamshedpur, Tata steel mill, 17
Japan, 20, 130; protectionism, 53
Jute, 78

Kenya, 105, 106, 128; coffee, 102; export locations, 135; flower exports, 73; outsourcing pioneers, 100; tea, 62, 85; vegetable exports, 80-1
Keynes, J.M., 71, 83
Khruschev, Nikita, 119-20
'knowledge economy', 14
Kolkata, India, 31
Kraft Foods, 98; pressure on, 100
Kyrgyzstan, 18; *per capita* incomes, 16

Lagos Plan of Action, 36-8, 130, 134
Lake Chad, drying up, 19
landlocked countries, 18
Laos, 17-18
late payment pressure, 104
Latin America: farm size, 101; remote area poverty, 6; supermarkets, 125; trade diversification, 143
Least Developed Countries (LDCs), 14; Africa, 136; diversification reduction, 49; export prices fall, 43
Lebanon, remittances importance, 65
Liberia, 48
life expectancy, inequality of, 3, 14
London Metal Exchange's contracts, 69
low income food-deficit countries, FAO category, 22

Madagascar: nickel-cobalt deposits, 47; vanilla exports, 42, 62, 66, 70, 78, 81
Madhya Pradesh, malnourishment, 25
maize, 120, 124, 130, 143; bioethanol demand, 63; Southern Africa, 132
Make Poverty History, campaign, 1
Malaysia, 91; Economic Planning Unit, 53; price stabilization plan, 85; state economic planning, 54

Mali, 19, 128; cotton, 64; education lack, 23
malnutrition, 123; children, 25; *see also*, hunger
Mao Zedong, 17
marginal lands, poverty, 6
marketing boards, national agricultural, 31, 55, 95, 130
markets: entry problems, 109; fetishized, 55, 58; incomplete rural, 137
Mauritius, 130; EU sugar quota, 78, 145; sugar export quotas, 55
McCormick, USA, 42
Mercosur, 134
Michigan State University, 137
Microsoft, break-up threat, 111
migrant labour, Central American, 65
milk, 76, 127
millet, 9, 120, 124, 131-2; African production, 125
mineral-exporting countries, 48
Moldova, 18, 23-4; *per capita* incomes, 16; remittances importance, 65
Mongolia, 18-19
Morocco, vegetable exports, 82
Mozambique: alumina exports, 21; cashew nut exports, 49-50; sugar price, 78
Multi-Fibre Arrangement, 135

narcotics, cultivation incentive, 44
National Farmers Union, Canada, 23
National Health and Family Survey, India, 25
neo-colonialism, 142
Nepal, 17-18, 24
Nestlé, 98; 73, 97, 99
Neumann, 93
New International Economic Order, proposed, 142
Niger, 22, 131; terms of trade, 23; vegetable exports, 82
Nigeria, 20, 62, 126, 131; oil industry, 34; palm oil, 33; root crops, 125
Nixon, Richard M., 119
non-traditional commodities, 79-80, 106
'normal' standards, different perceptions of, 16
North-Korea, closed economy, 44

OECD (Organization of Economic Cooperation and Development), 134
oil, 21, 34, 47, 64, 90; price, 61-2, 66, 89

oligopsonies, 112, 145
OPEC (Organization of the Petroleum Exporting Countries), 84, 88-9, 91, 119
Ottoman Empire, the, 34
outsourced production, 97, 100; supermarkets, 98; TNC outgrower schemes, 96
Oxfam, 70, 93, 99, 105

Pakistan, emigrant labour, 65
palm oil, 33, 85, 90, 143; biofuel use, 79; Indonesian plantations, 102
Papua-New Guinea, 42; vanilla, 78
Paraguay, soya monoculture, 103
pesticides, 102, 107
Philippines, 24; emigrant women, 65
plantains, 124
plantations, colonial, 31
Poland, emigrant labour, 65
Portugal, commercial expansion, 19
poverty: African concentration, 16; Bangladesh, 8; definition over-simplification, 14; measurement differences, 7; reduction emphasis, 56; remote areas, 6, 18; rural, 148
Poverty Reduction Strategy Papers, 56
Prebisch, Raúl, 72
primary commodities: exports dependence, 20, 30; supply control, 15
Procter & Gamble, 114; profit margins, 97
protectionism, 137, 142
Putin, Vladimir, 53

quotas, export, 86, 88, 145

recession, 1980s, 89-90
regional trade, 130, 133, 147; currency, 136; food, 131; obstacles, 135
remittances, 65; importance of, 20
remote areas, 148; poverty, 18-19; transport needs, 133
Rhodes, Cecil, 140
Ricardo, David, 133
rice, 42, 124, 127; African deficit, 120; price volatility impact, 63
risk, poor people's vulnerability, 8
Romania, 23
Royal African Company, 30
rubber, 85, 87, 90
rural crisis, global, 5, 29
Rural Poverty Report, IFAD, 6

Russia: economic nationalism, 53; socialist revolution, 141

São Tomé & Principe, 77
Sahel, the, 19; Sahelian route, 18
Samarkand, 19
Sarkozy, Nicolas, 114
Scott, Lee, 114
Second World War, post, 141
Sender, John, 7
Serbia, remittances importance, 65
Sherman Act, USA, 111
Sierra Leone, 48, 77
Silk Road, 18
Singapore, 79, 144
Singer, Hans, 72
slavery, economic system, 30-1; end of, 34
small countries, disadvantages, 17, 19, 77
smallholders, dryland areas, 6
Smith, Adam, 34, 72, 110-12
social exclusion (destitution), 8
Solomon Islands, 18; *per capita* incomes, 16
sorghum, 9, 120, 124, 131-2; African production, 125
South Africa, 95; farmers' risks, 105
South Korea, 20, 53; authoritarian stage, 51
South-South trade, 143
soya, 76, 94, 120; biofuel use, 79; monoculture, 103
Spain, commercial expansion, 19
speculation, financial, 67-9
Sri Lanka, tea, 85
Standard Oil, 115; break-up, 111
standards, food: imposition of, 135; private certification, 109; universal private, 108
state the: budget restrictions, 57; planning role, 54; role reduction, 50
Sterling currency area, 142
stock-control processes, 86
structural adjustment policies, 15, 36-7, 45, 50, 55, 71, 88-9, 95, 118; era of, 57
Sub-Saharan Africa, 43; food importing, 118; milk imports, 128; trade barriers, 136; vegetable exports, 81-2
subsidies, Northern farmers, 64, 72, 78
sugar, 120; biofuel use, 79; cane, 143; EU quotas, 76, 78; exporting countries, 77; slave economy, 30-1; US quotas, 123
supermarkets: bargaining power, 73, 94, 105-6, 113; chain expansion, 95; food standards imposition, 108; Latin America, 125; profit margins, 97, 99, 103; sales monitoring, 96; supply chain control, 24
supplier-managed inventory, 98
supply, agricultural inelasticity, 67
supply chain, corporate power, 24, 86, 94-7; key points, 73, 83
supply management, 85; corporate, 89, 93, 110; ICAs, 87; non-corporate, 88; producer-led, 90-1; public, 83; varieties, 84-5
Swaziland, EU sugar quota, 78
sweet potatoes, 9, 124, 127; African production, 125
Switzerland, 20

Taiwan, economic planning, 54
Tajikistan, 18
Tanzania, 127; farmers, 9
tariffs, 86; cost of reductions, 57; reduction insistence, 35, 38
Tata, 17
tea, 72, 76, 87, 118; export quotas system, 84; global producer discussions, 85; managed international period, 83; prices, 62
terms of trade, 21, 43
Tesco, supermarket chain, 103, 114; government lobbying support, 112
Thailand, 91; supermarkets, 101
Thatcher, Margaret, 45
Timbuktu, 18
tin, 90; price collapse, 64; *see also*, International Tin Agreement
tobacco, 72, 76; subsidies, 78
Tonga, remittances importance, 65
tourism, 21; import requirements, 45
trade: liberalization consequences, 15, 49; maritime, 18
trade unions, pressures against, 110
transport: costs, 19; food exports, 79
Trevelyan, Charles, 32
'triangular trade', 31
'trickle down' theory, 133
tropical logs, price fall, 64
tungsten, 90
Turkey, structural adjustment loan, 37

Uganda, 126; oil discovery, 47; vanilla, 42, 78

UK (United Kingdom), 101; agriculture, 145; coffee retail price, 76; corruption, 51; Empire and Commonwealth preference system, 14; farms, 23-4, 73; Japanese car companies, 45; migrant labour, 65; Monopolies Commission, 111; *see also*, Britain

Ukraine, 23

UN (United Nations), 141; Centre for Transnational Corporations (closed), 113; Conference on Trade and Development (UNCTAD), 21, 62, 70-1, 89-90, 94, 107, 120, 137, 142; Development Programme, 2, 14, 16, 20; FAO, see Food and Agriculture Organization; Millennium Development Goals, 56

urban slums, 6

urban-rural divide, 24

USA, (United States of America, 35, 73, 143); anti-trust laws, 111, 113; bioethanol, 63; cotton subsidies, 72, 78; food exports, 118; 'food weapon' use, 119; industrialization protectionism, 51, 53; migrant labour, 65; sugar quota, 123

USSR (Union of Soviet Socialist Republics, ex-): break-up, 23; food import dependency, 22, 118-20, 123; political liberalization, 51

value chains, global imperatives, 80

vanilla, 76, 78, 90; price collapse, 42-3, 49; price volatility, 66, 70

vegetable exports, 82

Venezuela, 143

vertical integration, food companies, 99

Vietnam, coffee, 48, 102

Volcafe, 93

Wade, Robert, 128

Wal-Mart, 95, 97, 114; ASDA subsidiary, 99, 113; power of, 104

Washington Consensus, 35-6, 'post'- 50, 56, 144

West Africa, cotton, 72

wheat, 127; futures exchange, 69; price movements, 61-3; subsidies, 72

Wilson, Woodrow, 141

women, agricultural labour, 8

World Bank, 8-9, 38, 58, 71, 126-7, 134, 142-3; Berg Report, 35-7, 50, 55, 57, 83, 148; corruption in, 52; creation, 141; export-led model, 36; 'good governance' rhetoric, 50-2; International Development Association, 56; Mozambique interference, 49; 1980s policy shift, 29, 35, 50; Pearson Report, 2; policy role, 37; *World Development Report* 1986, 39

WTO (World Trade Organization), 76, 106-7, 113, 134, 142; African Group, 85; Agreement on Agriculture, 144; Doha Round, 38, 64, 149; Seattle Conference, 148; TRIMS agreement, 45; TRIPS agreement, 46

yams, 124

Yemen, 20

Zambia, 62, 105, 108; copper from, 33, 47

Zanzibar, cloves, 81